Orgasm

Gateway to enlightenment

NIRVANA

Orgasm

ALSO BY NIRVANA

The Silent Path
The Greatest Love Story Never Told
In Search of I
The Ocean in a Drop
The Whirling Dervish
Where the Hell are You Going?
Storm Before the Calm
Dancing with Shadows

Copyright © 2024 Nirvana Foundation
All rights reserved.

ISBN: 978-1-962685-08-5

No part of this publication may be reproduced, distributed, or transmitted in any form or by any means, including photocopying, recording, or other electronic or mechanical methods, without the prior written permission of the publisher, except as permitted by U.S. copyright law.

For permission requests, contact
Nirvana Foundation
Email: info@nirvana.foundation
Website: www.nirvana.foundation

Acknowledgment

The whole universe has to come together to move a single blade of grass. This book would not have been possible without the support of everything that has ever happened. I am especially grateful to my students, who record, transcribe, edit, and publish my talks.

Orgasm

Table of Contents

Introduction	9
The Alchemy of Sexuality	13
The Purity of Sex	14
The Energy of Sex	16
What Happened?	19
Celebrate, not Celibate	27
Sex is Natural	28
Brahmacharya, Naturally	33
The Art of Pleasure	39
First Impressions	40
She Enjoys Sex	44
Sex is Profound	54
The Soul of Sexuality	59
Who am I?	60
Global Weirding	65
No Gender	67
Self-Pleasure	77
Why Masturbate?	78
Awakening Through Masturbation	86

The Clitoral Network	91
Together in Spirit	99
What is "Natural"	100
Individual Preferences	103
Life is Fluid	115
Meditation and Sex	118
Divine Harmony	123
The "Original Sin"	123
Sex isn't Just for Reproduction	132
Law of Attraction	137
From Sacred to Scandalous	145
The "Devolution" of Sex	146
Experience No Experience	150
The Monotony of Monogamy	154
The Harem Fantasy	167
Public vs. Private	172
Sensual Meditation	179
Sex is Inside	180
Intercourse	187
The Orgasm of Enlightenment	192
About Nirvana	201

Introduction

Welcome to a transformative exploration where the paths of sexuality and spirituality converge, leading us toward a deeper understanding of consciousness itself. "Orgasm - Gateway to Enlightenment," invites us to reevaluate what we know about the most primal and mystical aspects of human experience - sex.

Sex is not merely an act; it is an opening, a profound gateway to the depths of who we are and what we can become. It is both the most common of our desires and the most powerful portal through which we can encounter our true selves and the cosmos. Yet, in our modern world, sex often appears misunderstood, wrapped in contradictions and controversies, and laden with social taboos and ancient moralities that no longer serve us.

In these pages, we embark on a journey that moves beyond the superficial treatments of sex prevalent in both our media and personal conversations. We dive into the alchemical powers of sexuality - how it shapes us, what it reveals about us, and how it can, indeed, transform us. We question the age-old conflict between the flesh and the spirit, challenging the notion that to be spiritual, one must deny the physical. Instead, we celebrate sexuality as a vital force, an inherent aspect of our spiritual journey.

Why are we irresistibly drawn to sex? How does it connect us not only to our own bodies and minds but also to another soul? How can understanding our sexual selves lead us to greater spiritual heights? These are some of the questions this book seeks to answer. We will explore the essence of pleasure, not just in its immediate gratifications but as a profound interaction that can enhance intimacy, understanding, and connection with one's partner.

Moreover, we discuss the role of self-pleasure, often shunned and shadowed by misconceptions, recognizing it as a path to personal enlightenment - a way to explore the depths of our own being without shame or guilt. We will also navigate through the misconceptions surrounding different sexual orientations and relationships, urging a more compassionate and inclusive understanding that respects the spiritual potential in all forms of love.

This book also addresses the more controversial aspects of sexuality - its misuse, the fantasies it spawns, and its role in power dynamics. We understand these as expressions of repressed selves, unexplored desires, and unresolved conflicts. By bringing these to light, we hope to uncover pathways to heal and integrate these aspects, transforming them from sources of confusion and conflict into opportunities for growth and enlightenment.

"Orgasm - Gateway to Enlightenment" is not just a book; it is an invitation to a more expansive view of life where every act of love, every moment of pleasure, every encounter with desire is an opportunity to meet the divinity within and around us. Let us begin this sacred journey together, with open hearts and minds, ready to transform the energy of our deepest drives into the light of higher awareness. Join us as we uncover the secrets of sexuality and spirituality, intertwined in the eternal dance of creation.

Orgasm

THE ALCHEMY OF SEXUALITY

What is sex exactly? Why are we so drawn to it?

Sex is not just a word; it's a whole library. To understand sex, you must grasp many things. When something is unmistakably present in all things, it has a unique identity that stands apart, with an unmistakable flavor and an unmissable fragrance. Such a phenomenon must be existential, not merely human. What we recognize as human is just a rearrangement of familiar experiences - experiences known to the body and mind. Desires like traveling, eating good food, or resting are understandable. But the desire for sex is a mysterious and powerful force beyond human comprehension.

It is no surprise then, that sex is the least understood and most misunderstood of human experiences. The tragedy of humanity lies in this misunderstanding of sex. There is no other "fall" of Man; this misunderstanding defines our downfall. Without grasping the essence of what drives us, where we come from, what we long for, or our origins and destinies, how can we truly know ourselves or understand life? Thus, sex is not merely an exercise in pleasure. Pleasure is just a small part of sex - the part we recognize and are drawn to because it ends in an enjoyable experience. Yet, this experience is something we do not fully understand but are irresistibly drawn to. The ridiculousness of the act post-completion, the dehumanizing aspect of losing oneself so completely, dropping the ego, and entering the act as naked and vulnerable as a child, is baffling. In sex, you are both present and absent; it is the only place where you are willing to lose yourself entirely to find yourself anew. Sex is both the nourisher and the destroyer of your being.

THE PURITY OF SEX

It does not matter who you are or what you have accomplished, whether you are a king or a beggar, a sinner or a saint. Everyone approaches sex in the same way. You cannot bring your dignity, respect, or self-identity into the exploration of sex. You cannot accommodate both yourself and the desire for sex. That is why it is such a mysterious force - "I am willing to drop everything I hold valuable." If only a person could truly see themselves in the act of sex, they would instantly realize that they are witnessing someone else, not their usual self. There's an immediate shift in identity. It's like entering a beautiful, sacred temple. Before entering, you must cleanse yourself and leave your sandals outside. You cannot enter if you are in a state of unrest, anger, frustration, or jealousy.

What is the objective of entering this temple? You want to be in the presence of something higher, deeper, something greater. That's why there's detachment - you drop all you have accumulated because you know it means nothing in the presence of something greater. You drop all and then enter the temple. Observe how people enter what they recognize as their sacred space, whether it's a temple, church, or mosque. Something changes in their body language, in the way they move, in the way they think. Just the idea of entering a sacred space transforms them.

The same happens with sex. The very thought of it, the idea of it, awakens the child within you. It is only the child inside that can explore the purity of sex. The adult in you can only distort it. The adult is the mind, which knows nothing about sex. If it tries to understand, it only perverts and complicates it. But the child inside intuitively knows something about sex, because it is born through that process. Every cell in the body is a sex cell.

The process of birth, which cannot occur without sex, is continuously happening within the human body. Parts of us are constantly being born while others fade away, all fueled by the same sexual energy. Deep down, the body is already in communion with sex, merely longing for something it inherently knows. The mind may not understand sex, but the body is immersed in it, breathing and living it. This explains the body's craving for sex - it's like a fish craving water. It is a misunderstanding that transforms sex into merely an act or activity. When you truly understand sex, you realize it is intrinsic to your very nature. This understanding reveals who you are; it shapes your identity and the way you view life.

The Energy of Sex

Sexual energy is fundamental - it is the sole energy that multiplies and manifests as form and life, a pure ocean of aliveness. Our longing isn't for something external but to fully experience ourselves. Sex is a journey towards the ultimate destination of understanding oneself, often recognized during an orgasm - a moment when all false identities dissolve. This moment transcends expression because there is no one to experience it. An orgasm isn't just an experience; it represents the cessation of all experiences. It is a brief merger of your individual identity with the ultimate identity, experienced as bliss - a transcendental state indescribable by the body or mind. This profound enticement is what draws us to sex. If we view sex merely as an activity, it seems nonsensical. We must see it as a journey to understand its purpose: who the traveler is, where they are going, and what their destination is. This perspective is the only way to truly comprehend sex.

We have misunderstood sex because we have become too obsessed with its physical activities. We focus so much on what we see during sex that we miss what is actually happening. We haven't gone deeply into how it dissolves identity, resolves inner conflicts, or reconciles experiences. A lot is happening during sex - your inner universe undergoes a turbulent transformation. Sex is the only endeavor where you traverse the entire length and breadth of your being in just a few moments. This rapid exploration doesn't occur in any other activity, not even in meditation. Meditation requires months, even years, to journey from one aspect of your being to another; it's a slow and gradual process. In contrast, during sex, you explore the depths of your being in unimaginable ways. No part of you remains hidden; you are utterly exposed and open to everything that occurs. This complete exposure is why all your emotions are released and expressed through sex. It isn't sex that makes you angry or jealous, nor does it bring out your dominant or submissive traits. These emotions arise because you are overwhelmed by your mind and ego. You become something you are not meant to be.

Sex is the washroom where you cleanse yourself of all that you have accumulated and become. It is your only refuge in this life, the only place where you can see everything you've become and attempt to rid yourself of it. This is why sex is a cathartic process - it provides emotional, psychological, and physical healing. It is not merely a craving or desire. If you perceive sex as just a desire, you will try to restrict it because this one desire overpowers all others. Given a choice between good sex and good food, or between good sex and comfort, you would choose good sex. There's nothing that can surpass the craving for sex. Hence, it must be condemned, encaged, and approached with caution because you do not understand the totality of sex. You don't see how deep its roots go; you only see the branches and leaves. You recognize the immense influence it has on your life but not its true power. The only way to deal with it, then, is through condemnation. And that is what we have done.

WHAT HAPPENED?

Over the last several centuries, humanity has only known sex through condemnation. It has not entered this sacred space with reverence, openness, or child-like curiosity. Something changed in the human journey that altered our approach to sex. The changes we see around us - the world has become more chaotic, confusing, and detached and individuals are more lost, angry, jealous, and frustrated - can all be traced back to our altered approach to sex.

A few things are important to understand. While the present moment ultimately governs how you understand and connect with yourself, and while your current state of mind determines your perception of life, you are also a product of human evolution. You carry the collective experiences of the past within your memory, residing in both mind and body. Therefore, without understanding your past and the pivotal moments when humanity started moving in certain directions, it's impossible to fully grasp such a universal phenomenon as sex.

Why is it necessary to look back in time to see if something went wrong? If everything were perfect, if our understanding of sex were complete, if sex were accepted as a part of life and seen as an expression of love, without perversion or condemnation, then nothing would have gone wrong. We look back because we know something has indeed gone wrong.

Our detachment and disconnected understanding of sex are reflected in all our activities, our level of happiness, and our connection with ourselves. It is reflected in how we treat people and animals, and in how we understand life. Fundamentally, do we see life as a glorious, magnanimous expression of love, or as a fallen state? It's all connected to sex. The easiest way to see that something has gone wrong is to observe how we approach sex. We often engage in sex in a hurry, which is the first noticeable sign of our misunderstanding.

You cannot compare human sexuality with animal sex; these are two completely different things. That is another area where our understanding has completely failed. We cannot equate our sexual experiences with those of animals because, for us, sex is so much more than reproduction. This is what separates us from animals: we have identified sex as the primary energy that gives rise to creativity, love, compassion, and all the best qualities we yearn for. Animals do not view sex in this way; for them, it is merely a process through which they multiply.

We are not relaxed in sex. We don't approach it with a sense of reverence, with a sense of acceptance, because somewhere deep down, we know that we are prisoners who are enjoying sex as a luxury. It is not something that we deserve. This comes from social conditioning - the undeniable feeling that you are experiencing something that you're not supposed to. That is why sex is always an activity that is done behind closed doors. You don't see it out in the open. Why not? What is inherently wrong with sex? Animals have sex on the outside, they don't go to one corner to have sex. Animals that live in communities, in groups, never go somewhere else. They don't care who's watching because there's no condemnation of sex. There are no negative feelings attached to it. For them, it is simply an activity that is an extension of their being.

But look at human beings. We have to hide it. We have to do it in secret. It is such a common practice that we think sex has to be done in private, but we never question why. We have condemned everything sex is and everything that comes out of sex, including our bodies. We don't view our bodies as an extension of our true being. We live with our bodies with a sense of detachment; we look at them in shame. This is the tragic reality of the human race. It is this misunderstanding of sex, this perversion of sex that is the root of all our internal conflicts. You can see this everywhere.

If an individual is finding it hard to stand on a stage, look into the eyes of his fellow human beings, and say something, where does this come from? What is he afraid of? He's afraid of being judged, but what are they judging? He has not even spoken. He has not even shared his mind. Then what is he afraid of? If he were to stand naked without any clothes, would he be comfortable? He might have something very important to share. He knows that people will understand what he is trying to say and he will get their appreciation, but imagine if he were to just stand naked in front of them, doing nothing. He has not committed any crime. He's not done anything wrong. He is just standing there. Now, that is enough to cause discomfort and create conflict inside him.

This is what we have done to humanity. We have divided people to such an extent that there is hardly a moment when one can simply be oneself. If you are judged, condemned, or criticized for something you have done, that criticism can be accepted. However, if you are condemned or judged for who you are, that is what we call racism. You judge someone before even understanding them, based solely on preconceived notions. In this sense, we are all racist. We judge as soon as we see a person. We don't consider what that person has done or what they are about to do. Just the fact that you look a certain way, just because you have certain body parts that you did not choose - these were not choices you made at a store. You were born with them. You did not choose to be a man or a woman. And yet, everything about your body belongs to you. Nevertheless, this very body has become the greatest source of conflict.

What should be a vehicle that transports you from one experience to another, accommodating you gracefully and not interfering with your experience of life, merely existing as a vehicle, has now become the biggest point of conflict. It is not you who is being judged, but rather this vehicle. Thus, wherever you go, people do not truly care about you; they are only concerned with the vehicle you are using. Clearly, something has gone wrong.

We must look back in time to understand what went awry. Unnaturalness has infiltrated our very being, becoming part of our essence. There was a time when sex was natural. We were liberated, understanding what it meant to be truly free - a freedom that required no reasoning, no justification. A freedom so expansive that you could engage in intimate acts under the open sky in the presence of family members, friends, and your community without any issue. This was a freedom without limitations or bounds, a concept utterly foreign to the imprisoned part of you that knows only constrained intimacy. In a sense, intimacy is a means of momentarily breaking these shackles, which is why you feel such urgency, for you are a captive. There is a beautiful poem by D.H. Lawrence that encapsulates this perfectly. He writes:

Wild things in captivity
While they keep their own wild purity
won't breed, they mope, they die.

All men are in captivity.
Active with captive activity,
and the best won't breed, though they don't know why.

The great cage of our domesticity
kills sex in a man, the simplicity
of desire is distorted and twisted awry.

And so, with bitter perversity,
gritting against the great adversity,
the young ones copulate, hate it, and want to cry.

Sex is a state of grace.
In a cage, it can't take place.
Break the cage, then start in and try.

To truly understand the deep, beautiful essence of sex, we need to first understand what has trapped us: who or what has locked us up, what our chains are made of, and the framework within which we view sex. Without grasping these constraints, we can't fully appreciate this profound phenomenon.

Orgasm

Celebrate, not Celibate

Does one have to be celibate to pursue a path of spirituality?

Wherever you look, there is sex. It has broken through all boundaries. Now, you don't even know how to separate your sexual desires from your worldly desires because all your desires are sexual. Even the so-called worldly desires are merely disguised sexual desires. Celibacy is cruel and inhuman at all levels, including temporary celibacy, social celibacy, and celibacy pursued for the sake of obtaining something else. Purposeful celibacy is all repression. Far from helping you grow spiritually, it will make you more focused on sexuality. It will make it harder for you to divert your attention away from your desires. It will draw you deeper into a world of desires.

Celibacy had its place in society at a certain time under certain conditions, but those conditions have changed. Our minds have changed. Our understanding of life has changed. We are now much more knowledgeable about our bodies and minds. Our awareness of what sex is, what reproduction entails, how a child is produced, and what birth involves has grown. We understand the process scientifically, so there is no necessity to blindly hold on to a dead religious idea of celibacy. The only thing we need to be aware of is how much of our energies are being dedicated to sexual desires. As a society, as a community, if we aim to liberate human beings, to offer them more opportunities to pursue a higher path, to allow human energies to find different, creative, constructive expressions through which they can acquire more knowledge, wisdom, and understanding, we only need to understand why our minds are so occupied with sex. The moment we see that it is our imposed restrictions on sex that are making us more focused on it, we will realize that the direction in which we need to move is not towards celibacy but towards the opposite. We need to begin to free individuals from artificially imposed restrictions on sex.

Sex is Natural

Once sex is viewed as something natural, it becomes just that - natural. It won't occupy all your time or become your biggest obsession. It will be one of many desires. You crave good food, comfort, and the momentary pleasures of life; sex will simply be another craving. There is absolutely no problem in accommodating your spiritual desires or a quest to know yourself amidst these other desires because no single desire dominates your life. These are all natural life processes.

In Sanskrit, there is a word for celibacy: "Brahmacharya." It's composed of two words: "Brahma" and "acharya." Brahma is the ultimate reality, a state of being where you are above and beyond all desires, having become pure consciousness, and pure aliveness. "Acharya" means practice. Consider the beauty of this word - Brahmacharya means practicing consciousness, practicing a higher state of being, an awakened state.

However, this word may not resonate with someone who is lost in his mind, or lost in the desires of his body. It only makes sense from an awakened state. Once you have navigated through the desires of your mind and body, understood enough about yourself, and learned how to distance yourself from your thoughts, you experience a state of purity. From that state, whatever you do, you are living as an expression of Brahman, as an expression of pure consciousness. From this state, your craving for sex dissipates. You are no longer dependent on sex. Your self-identity is not tied to sex.

Once in a while, you can entertain thoughts of sex, but it's nowhere near being the force that drives your life. It is just a tiny part of your life, and that too, only if you want it. If you don't want it, if you choose to drop it entirely, you can. That is Brahmacharya, where you are so engrossed, so absorbed in Brahman that there is no need to crave sex. Now, imagine trying to impose this as a rule on someone who knows nothing about it, someone who is unfamiliar with meditation, who knows nothing about internal bliss. How can you impose it as a rule? Yet, that is what religions have done. The idea is beautiful: to live beyond sexual desires, to not crave sex. Yes, it's a wonderful state to be in. But it is a state that you must reach on your own. Nobody can give it to you. However, if you walk into any ashram in India, the first thing that is imposed on you is Brahmacharya, a state that requires years of understanding and practice, yet is imposed as a rule. Now, what happens? Because you are unnaturally, artificially trying to suppress it, it starts finding its expression in other things. Even a thought of a woman, even the idea of sex, disturbs you.

There is a story told of King Vishwamitra which, in a way, explains how inseparable the ideas of sex, children, and reproduction are, and why such emphasis is placed on celibacy.

Vishwamitra was a great king and warrior. One day, he decides to pursue a spiritual path. He wishes to leave his worldly life behind and become a sage. He starts practicing meditation, moves away from his kingdom, and becomes an ascetic in the forest. The gods see this and decide to disturb his penance. For some reason, gods keep doing this - no one knows why, but they seem interested in interfering with one's sex life, whether you're having more sex or abstaining from it. This, in a way, says more about us than about the gods.

So, it is said that the gods decided to intervene and destroy his penance. They send a celestial nymph, supposed to be the most beautiful, drop-dead gorgeous, stunning woman - no man can deny her. That is how beautiful she is; the very definition of beauty. After all, the gods have created her, so naturally, she would be beautiful. When Vishwamitra sees Menaka, he forgets all about his penance. He forgets his path, his abstinence, and his celibacy, and marries her, eventually having children.

However, as it naturally happens - it doesn't matter whether you are with someone beautiful - after a while, desires wane, and reality sets back in. This is exactly what happened to Vishwamitra. After years of marriage and family life, he realizes, "I have been tricked. I need to return to my celibate ways." He then decides to leave his family and become a monk again.

This story illustrates the immense strength required, even for a man like Vishwamitra - a great warrior and king accustomed to fighting his enemies - to resist a simple sexual desire. Ultimately, he had to return to celibacy to pursue enlightenment.

This story is traditionally told to emphasize the necessity of celibacy; otherwise, you risk entanglement in samsara, getting married, having children, and deviating from the spiritual path. However, if this same story were retold today, it might go very differently.

Imagine Vishwamitra meditating deeply in the forest. The gods decide to disturb his penance and send Menaka. Vishwamitra opens his eyes, sees Menaka, and they have sex. He uses protection because he knows he does not want children - it's mutually agreed upon. They acknowledge each other's needs; Menaka, created for this purpose, surely craves sex too. After fulfilling their desires, they part ways. Vishwamitra then says, "I do not want children because I am focused on my enlightenment," and he returns to his meditation, eventually achieving enlightenment.

In this story, instead of fighting or making it a big deal, it's like saying, "I want to breathe, but I'm against breathing. I'll suppress it; I'll control it." Why? If only you can understand the consequences of sex, if you can intelligently approach it while still keeping your higher goal intact, there is absolutely no problem in accommodating sex. And by its very nature, once you know you can have sex, there are no artificially imposed rules, you won't be thinking about it all the time. It'll just be one other thing. As you go deeper into meditation, as you ascend spiritually, your desire for sex naturally reduces because your body is becoming more relaxed. It is touching those pleasure zones naturally. It is not stressed, anxious, or worried. Remember, sex is connected to all these states. The more anxious or disturbed you are, the more you want to release those energies, and the more you seek an outlet.

Brahmacharya, Naturally

When you start settling into your body naturally, when you start falling in love with your body, when you start accepting yourself more - which is all a natural progression in spirituality - your craving for sex diminishes. Now, without fighting sex, without trying to artificially curb it, you have naturally accommodated it as part of your life. And a day comes, perhaps without you even noticing, when sex is perfectly there as a tiny part of your life. And someday, it might even completely disappear without leaving any residue of its absence. You will not crave it; you will not miss it. It's gone, and you don't even notice it. That is the natural way of attaining a state of Brahmacharya. That is the natural way to become celibate. It is not about imposing celibacy but about finding joy and pleasure within yourself in such a way that there is no necessity to crave sex. Any approach, other than this natural way, will only make you more fixated on sex, potentially leading to more perversion.

A monk enters a monastery and takes a vow of celibacy, spending many years avoiding all temptations. One day, he is given the task of copying the ancient texts by hand. While in the cellar reviewing the originals, he suddenly bursts into tears and runs upstairs to the head monk, sobbing uncontrollably.

The head monk asks him, "Brother, what is the matter?"

The monk replies, "I checked the original manuscript... It says 'celebrate', not 'celibate'!"

Returning to the question: Can practicing celibacy or abstinence contribute to spiritual growth? No, it will actually contribute to your sexual growth. How do you approach sex intelligently? With awareness. Yes, it helps to not produce ten children. That's where your energy is being wasted - not in sex itself. There's no wastage of energy in sex unless you're engaging in it excessively. When approached moderately, sex actually replenishes your energy, relaxes your mind and body, and can even aid in your spiritual growth by alleviating some of the depression in your body. The waste of energy in sex occurs when you don't separate sex from family life or marriage.

Consider the trick of human society. In a way, human society is perfectly arranged to prevent enlightenment. How does it achieve this? Firstly, it insists on no sex until marriage. This has been the norm for a very long time. Boys and girls wait for marriage, consumed with anticipation. Now, how can you focus on spirituality, awareness, or consciousness when you're preoccupied with waiting for marriage? There goes your spiritual pursuit. Then, once you get married, you dive into sex. Subsequently, there's the restriction that you cannot have sex outside of marriage, and now your sex life becomes a source of frustration. You've been waiting your whole life, and now that you have experienced sex, your frustration only increases because, having known what sex is, you yearn to explore it further. You want to have more sex, but you're bound by the clear restriction that you cannot engage in sex outside of marriage. It's a perfect ploy to ensure that your mind remains fixated on sex and sex alone.

It is not surprising that the human mind is not filled with ideas of enlightenment. It is not a meditative mind; it's a sexual mind. We have tricked ourselves into spiritual ignorance, into being in bondage, in servitude. The way to go beyond this is to understand sex, not to suppress it. It is to accommodate it as part of your spiritual growth, to use it, and to incorporate it into your spiritual journey as a useful aid. When it is no longer necessary, it will naturally drop - you don't have to consciously force it. You will start using it less and less, and eventually, you will have gone beyond the craving for sex. That is when you will have attained a state of being free from sexual desires. Becoming free of sexual desires is not the starting point of a spiritual journey; it is the endpoint. When you reverse this, you completely misunderstand the process and subscribe to the mistaken rule that sex is opposed to spirituality, that thoughts of sex are against becoming spiritual, and that it is a sin. Now, what happens?

Imagine if you have progressed significantly on the spiritual path. You've spent months, even years, dedicatedly practicing meditation. Then one day, a temptation appears, and you lose control. You have sex. What happens then? There's so much guilt that you feel you have failed, that your meditation did not help you move away from this desire. You might abandon meditation, saying, "It is not working; it's not for me." You would use that one act as an anchor to return to a sexual life. Guilt is a very powerful force. Once you are trapped in guilt, forget about spirituality; you cannot even live a normal life. Sex has become a perfect device to induce guilt in the human mind.

The way to grow spiritually is to accept sex as a natural part of life, to recognize the force that it is, and to move beyond the guilt of sexual desires. That, in itself, is spiritual growth. Understanding sex itself can make you more spiritual. Moving beyond the guilt associated with sex can make you spiritual. After that, it's only a matter of time before you reach a perfect understanding of life.

Orgasm

THE ART OF PLEASURE

How can I enhance sexual pleasure for myself and my partner?

There are a few important things to understand: There is a clear difference between a man and a woman as far as sexuality is concerned. We might be similar in many aspects as creatures of the same species. As expressions of one life, there are a lot of similarities. But sexuality is where a man becomes a man and a woman becomes a woman. If you simply assume that you know your partner just because you've lived with them, fought with them, or had sex with them, you would be missing out on the main objective of sex, which is to understand each other fully and to know someone intimately. Knowing is not just intellectual. It is not even just physical; knowing extends so far that when you truly know someone, you are actually knowing yourself - and when you truly know yourself, you're knowing the other. Sex is the act through which you want to know everything there is to know about yourself as well as your partner. The general assumption is, "Oh, I already know my partner. That's why I'm having sex. I'm not having sex with a stranger." But do you really know?

In her book, "Mating in Captivity," Esther Perel says this: *Many of the couples who come to therapy imagine that they know everything there is to know about their mate. "My husband doesn't like to talk." "My girlfriend would never flirt with another man. She's not the type." "My lover doesn't do therapy." Why don't you just say it? I know what you're thinking." "I don't need to give her lavish presents. She knows I love her."*

I try to highlight for them how little they have seen, urging them to recover their curiosity and catch a glimpse behind the walls that barricade the other.

First Impressions

There is a natural tendency in a committed relationship to quickly reach a saturation point of knowing. Why? Because you know your partner more than anybody else. That gives the impression that you know everything about them. It is hard for you to accept that you don't know your partner. Firstly, it undermines your intelligence. It puts you in a zone of uncertainty to even entertain the idea that you're living with someone you don't yet fully understand. Forget about fully understanding - once you start trying to understand the real meaning of understanding someone, you will see that what you know about them is so little. And many things you know about each other are not even real, not even true. During the initial phase of a relationship, human beings hide their true nature. They don't reveal themselves. They don't expose themselves. They want to present the best possible image of themselves, out of the fear of rejection.

Most of what you know about each other is simply a sales pitch: "This is who I am. This is what I was." You both are marketing each other, physically, and emotionally. You have not honestly looked into each other. And that is why many marriages fail, because only when you start looking inside do you realize, "Oh, this is something else. This is not what I was looking for," and that's when all the conflicting arguments arise. "You were not like this" or "I know what you're thinking" - the clash between expectations and reality. It is not that you were trying to deceive each other, it's just that you were so infatuated with the idea of being with someone that you totally ignored them. You are filled with your own imagination of someone else.

It's interesting, in therapy sessions when people are asked about what was the first thing that drew them to their partner, what attracted them to each other -

the kind of reasons they give are so flimsy that there is no way you can build a relationship solely on those reasons. At most, you can have a one-night stand based on those reasons. Things like, "I loved their hair," "I loved their smile," "I loved their sense of humor," "she was gorgeous," or "I loved the way he laughed." The peculiarity is that, more often than not, it's only one reason; everything else is sidelined. There is no evaluation of what you like and what you don't like. What you don't like is not even visible. You keep ignoring it just so that you don't miss out on something you like. This is a natural flaw in how we like or dislike something. It's always the first thing, and that's why there is some truth in the statement that the first impression is the best impression. It's really what connects immediately - the first thing, and that is what you hold on to. That is what you look for more and more, and you ignore all the others.

It's only when you start exploring each other, really getting to know each other, that you'll see just how different you both are. Being different is essential; that's why you were attracted to each other. People who are exactly alike don't attract each other. That immediate attraction, that instant connection, doesn't just happen. It's inherent in the very nature of attraction that two people are different. And understanding one another is a lifelong journey. Once you let go of the assumption that you already know everything, then you can truly begin to explore.

Now, when you ask, "How can I change the way I approach sex to make it more pleasurable for both myself and my partner?" what you're really asking is, "How can I deepen my understanding of myself and my partner through sex?" Pleasure naturally follows from a deeper connection and understanding. If you explore human sexuality, you'll see that the deeper the connection, the more invested you become in the prospect of being with someone for the long haul. When thoughts of sharing each other's lives come into the picture, the quality of sex transforms, as opposed to it being solely about pleasure in the moment.

When there is no emotional connection, when there is no deeper existential connection, sex remains superficial. This is one of the significant divides between men and women. For a woman, sex is seventy percent emotional and only thirty percent physical. However, for a man, it's exactly the opposite. Because of his impulsive and quick sexuality by design, a man often sees sex as primarily for his pleasure, not for giving pleasure. This perception has been further complicated by societal structures that have overly nurtured his ego, to the extent that he often forgets that sex is more about giving than taking.

Many men have actually forgotten how to give pleasure. They neglect the importance of pleasuring their partners, focusing solely on their own gratification. It's as if they use the woman solely for their own pleasure, evident in their approach to sex, their language when discussing it, and how quickly they engage and disengage from it.

She Enjoys Sex

For women, it's an entirely different story. There has been an ongoing conspiracy against women's sexuality for a long time. It's evident that men have feared women's sexuality and have attempted to suppress it in various ways. Since culture is mostly shaped by men for men, the narratives and research explaining sex and the differences between men and women often favor men. Sadly, this is often overlooked, especially by men who accept these narratives as truth.

If you were to ask a man about a woman's desire for sex compared to his own, he would likely say hers is lower, without hesitation. He might think, "I want sex all the time, but she's not interested at all." Here lies the greatest misunderstanding. Women are just as interested in sex, if not more so, than men. However, throughout history, women's sexuality has been condemned to the point where a woman expressing her sexual desires is labeled as immoral. She's branded as promiscuous or sinful - a woman who simply acknowledges her desire for sex is deemed disloyal. Her role is seen as solely to satisfy her husband's needs. If she has her own desires, she's seen as betraying her relationship.

And that's precisely why, if you examine it closely, you'll notice that there are cultures where men are permitted to have multiple wives, but you will find very few, if any, cultures where a woman has the right to marry multiple men.

There is one particular experiment conducted by psychologists Russell Clark and Elaine Hatfield. It is famously known as the Clark-Hatfield study. It was conducted in 1989 on the campus of Florida State University. They sought to prove that women aren't as interested in sex as men. A good-looking woman was instructed to approach men and express her attraction to them, proposing sex. It's reported that a large percentage of the men - total strangers - agreed to have sex when approached by the woman. However, when a good-looking man approached a woman with the same proposition, not one woman agreed. This was presented as conclusive evidence that women are not interested in sex. But in reality, what it demonstrates is that women are often more discerning and cautious in their choices.

The fact that women aren't that interested in having sex with strangers doesn't imply they lack interest in sex. Their sexuality operates on a deeper level. They need to establish a connection with a man, to understand his character. They're not solely focused on the physical aspect, unlike men who often prioritize physical attraction and quick encounters. For a man, sex might feel like entering new and uncharted territory, driven by curiosity and adventure. He might think, "Let's see what happens; it could be good or bad, but let's explore." However, for a woman, sex is more like allowing a stranger into her home. She must proceed cautiously, making the right decision to avoid potential harm. This fundamental difference is crucial: Just as you wouldn't welcome anyone into your home without knowing them, a woman is selective about whom she allows into her intimate space. If she feels safe and comfortable, in a familiar environment, she may be more open to the experience. This contrast highlights how women approach sex with caution and discernment, whereas men, often driven by their desires and egos, may overlook these differences and fail to understand the complexity of a woman's perspective.

First and foremost, it's the woman who dominates sex, and it's she who must take charge. She needs to be on top, both literally and figuratively, because her sexuality is far broader and deeper. Pleasure in sex truly makes sense only when she can accommodate you, not the other way around. Why? Because fundamentally, deep down, you are also feminine. The essence of the body, the essence of sexuality, is feminine, not masculine.

Why do I say this? Consider the womb: Before the first trimester, the baby is essentially female. Every aspect of the embryo is feminine. There are no male characteristics, no distinguishing features that allow you to say, "Oh, this is a male baby." That differentiation occurs later in development.

It's been noted that both male and female genitals stem from the same embryonic tissue. While a woman's sexual organs develop inwardly, forming what you recognize as the clitoris, a man's develop outwardly as the penis. They are mirror images of each other, with a woman's clitoris not mirroring a man's penis, but rather the other way around. The outward growth occurs later, as an additional process that transforms the embryo into a male. However, most men aren't even familiar with the clitoris. If you were to suggest exploring the clitoral network, they might misinterpret it as something related to an electoral network. No, it's not an electoral network; it's the clitoral network.

Many men are astonishingly ignorant about the sexual anatomy of women. As Ian Kerner notes in "She Comes First,"

There are several questions men should ask themselves: Did you know that the clitoris consists of eighteen parts, all contributing to pleasure? Can you identify them? Were you aware that the majority of nerve endings responsible for the female orgasm are concentrated on the surface of the vulva, requiring no penetration for stimulation? Do you understand the various types of orgasms a woman can experience?

Man is thinking, "Are you talking about a woman or an alien?" He does not know all this. He does not know the complex nature of women's sexuality. He does not know that women's sexuality is not local - it is not restricted to one area, one part. Her whole body, every part of her being becomes sexual, and she has a dedicated sexual organ whose only purpose is pleasure - unlike men, whose sexual organ has to perform other functions, and whose primary job is not pleasure. It is involved in other things. Right there, you have to recognize the superiority of a woman's sexuality. She can have multiple orgasms. If you do not understand these things, if you do not understand that anything this deep, this complex, requires stimulation, requires time, it cannot just be a quick in and out, then there will always be a disconnect in the timing.

It's said that the problem doesn't lie with the fuse or the man's ability to ignite it. The real issue is that a woman's ignition cord is much longer than a man's. While his detonation happens much quicker, for her, the triggering has occurred, but she has to wait. Most men explode before a woman has any opportunity to express herself. This is the disconnect. Why is he finished so soon when she's just getting started?

Physically, men have somehow become conditioned to rush things. Moreover, mental stress, social pressures, and the stigma around sex being a guilty pleasure all contribute to not giving enough time. The single most significant change you can make in experiencing sex differently for yourself and your partner is to take your time - to listen, watch, be aware, and be fully involved. It's not about reaching a destination; it's about enjoying the journey. It's like a dance: The goal isn't to end the dance but to savor every step. Similarly, the objective of sex isn't just orgasm; you can't rush it. It has to unfold naturally, like a dance, and sex finds its true completion only when both man and woman experience orgasm together. That's when true union happens. Otherwise, you've simply used each other.

I'll go as far as saying that unless both the man and woman experience orgasm at the same time, the child resulting from that sexual union will be missing something. Just imagine a scenario where a female can't become pregnant without experiencing orgasm, similar to how a man cannot impregnate a woman without experiencing orgasm himself - it's physically impossible. At the moment of insemination, he's experiencing orgasm. However, a woman doesn't necessarily need to orgasm to conceive. She can still conceive without it. I believe this is a flaw in the human mechanism that has allowed for the suppression of women's sexuality.

Just imagine if it were impossible for a woman to become pregnant without experiencing orgasm. Then, the man would have to understand her sexuality. He would have to grasp what's happening within her and take the time to stimulate and pleasure her. Only then could he be certain that conception would occur. But because there's a disconnect there, something is missing in the child. The maternal side is missing, the feminine qualities are lacking, especially if it's a boy. It's all too quick, too focused on the man's pleasure, without considering the woman's needs and experience.

You need to understand that the qualities you identify in a child, both visible and invisible, stretch back to that moment of conception. In that moment of orgasm, you're offering more to the nourishment of that child than at any other time. While great emphasis is placed on genes inherited from ancestors - qualities passed down from parents, grandparents, and even further back - there's so much more that the child acquires. To begin with, the mother's mental and emotional state has a profound impact on the developing child, shaping not just their physical attributes but also their overall well-being.

Sex is that moment when the seed is being sown - the moment of conception. The more aware and conscious you are during this act, the more fertile the ground becomes to sow the seed of life - when you and your partner climax simultaneously, in a state of bliss, without the presence of ego. However, if you finish before your partner, you're sowing the seed of discontentment, giving birth to new life in an environment tainted by dissatisfaction.

It's a law of nature that different conditions exert different influences on life, whether we observe them or not. If there are two conditions - one where both partners are fully contented during conception, and another where only one is contented - just recognizing these differences is enough to understand that they will affect the child being produced. You might not understand how, but they will undoubtedly exert their influence.

That's the nature of life. You have to start by letting go of all assumptions, even if you've been intimate with your partner multiple times. You might understand something about their body, but you don't fully know them. There's so much more going on inside. That's why couples continue to have sex repeatedly. If you truly knew everything, if there was nothing left to explore, what would keep drawing you to each other? There's still something pulling you together, indicating that there's more to discover. Sex and knowing are intertwined; they're not separate. Sex loses its significance and allure when there's nothing left to learn from each other. When you know each other so completely that there's no energy moving towards understanding, sex loses its meaning.

That's why enlightenment or awakening changes your sexuality. The energy shifts, and the dynamics change. Yes, your mind may still entertain thoughts of sex, and may still crave physical beauty, because attraction is inherent in human nature. However, because you have gone deeply into self-exploration and know yourself fully, there's no longer a need to seek knowledge through another.

An enlightened individual has no craving for sex, no attachment to it. They can live perfectly contented without ever engaging in sexual activity. This state is only achievable after awakening, after enlightenment, because it's only in enlightenment that you fully know yourself. If you're not enlightened, then sex becomes a means of knowing, of exploring oneself and each other. So, you have to let go of your assumptions and approach sex with a sense of curiosity and playfulness. Leave your adult mind and ego at the door. It's not about what she can give you or what you can get from her. Sex is a different kind of game - it's not about winning or getting more; it's about giving, receptivity, and allowing things to unfold naturally. It's about taking your time above all else.

Yes, sex can be casual, but it's not inherently casual. You don't always have to approach sex with the intent to reach enlightenment or awakening. You can have sex simply for pleasure, but sex itself transcends mere pleasure. You shouldn't degrade it to just a means of deriving pleasure. The act itself should be treated as sacred and approached with love and reverence.

Whether you're engaging in a quick, mutually agreed-upon encounter or a more drawn-out experience, it's crucial never to forget that sex is not about using each other. It's a transcendental phenomenon - an expression of each other's inner divinity. It's a moment of vulnerability, where you're both naked in every sense - physically, emotionally, and spiritually. These are the moments when you can truly be yourself; the rest of the time, you're just wearing masks, unknown even to yourself.

In the purity of sex, you become mirrors reflecting each other's innermost selves. When these mirrors merge, the undivided consciousness is touched. You're not trying to create a union; the union already exists. You're simply attempting to dissolve the separateness.

Sex is Profound

Sex, the act itself, is essentially a means of erasing each other. Consider two individuals engaged in sex. What are they attempting to achieve? They're not seeking to enhance each other; rather, they're striving to erase each other's minds and body sensations. The ultimate experience occurs when both partners successfully erase each other completely - a moment where they've eliminated the distraction of the body, allowing them to meet for the first time.

It's only in the sexual union, at the moment of orgasm, that this profound meeting occurs. The rest of the time, they're merely attempting to connect.

This is why nothing can replace sex in a romantic relationship. While deep conversations and exchanges of love are significant, there's always a return to sex because it's where the true connection is forged. For a mind that hasn't explored meditation or gone deeply into self-inquiry, sex remains the primary means of connecting with another - a unique form of connection for minds and bodies lost in the world.

There's an entirely different pathway to transcending sexuality without even engaging in sex - it's a distinct process. These are the only two possibilities: Either following the path of Buddha, which entails no sexuality whatsoever - just pure inquiry and watchfulness, leading you to become yourself without relying on another body or external factors - or embracing sex as a method in itself.

Sex is a yogic practice, a technique, a complete method. When approached as a meditation, as a spiritual activity, it can transform one of the most engaging, pleasurable activities into a profound, awakening experience. You can transition from unconsciousness to consciousness, from ignorance to enlightenment, solely through sex. You don't need anything else, as long as you're willing to understand and approach it with the same reverence you would give to any teaching meant to deeply transform you.

For all of this transformation to occur, your sexuality must shift from your mind to your body. Particularly for men, sexuality tends to be concentrated in the mind. Due to various societal factors, such as perverted interpretations and misunderstandings of sex, as well as social ignorance, men have become creatures of sex in their minds. When sex enters the mind, it inevitably becomes distorted because the mind cannot directly experience it; instead, it imagines and fantasizes about it, often using it as a means of satisfying the ego.

For many men, sex is closely linked to their egos. This is why they are deeply hurt when denied sexual pleasure - nothing wounds a man's ego more than being denied sex, even by a partner with whom he has previously been intimate. This illustrates how sexuality has concentrated itself in the most unnatural of places: the mind. We can observe this by examining the way men live, how they arrange their lives, and where they find meaning - all of which often indicate a preoccupation with sex.

George was absolutely obsessed with the idea of an afterlife, but he was a skeptic at heart. He made his friend Rick promise that if Rick died first, he would find a way to let George know if there was life after death.

Not long after, Rick passed away. One night, George was woken up by Rick's voice. Startled, George asked, "Rick, is that you?"

"Yes, it's me," Rick's voice said.

"Wow! So there is life after death! What's it like?" asked George eagerly.

Rick replied, "Well, I wake up in the morning, have sex, eat breakfast, have sex, bask in the sun, have sex, eat lunch, have more sex..."

"Wait a minute," interrupted George, "are you in heaven?"

Rick responded, "No, I'm a rabbit in Arizona."

Sex is always on the mind. Sex is there, in your body and your mind, but when it is denied, when you're not getting it, that is when it becomes more of a mental obsession. Now, that is what pushes you towards sex unnaturally. You're not approaching it in the right way. You're in a hurry. You're trying to get something. That is where your aggression, fear, and disappointment in sex comes from. It's all connected to how closely your sexuality is related to your ego. If you truly want to understand your partner, if you are truly interested in enhancing each other's pleasure in sex, then you have to watch your ego. You have to be watchful of the mind before sex, during sex, and after sex. You have to watch the influence of the ego on your sex and keep the ego away. You don't have to specifically educate yourself on what sex is, and you don't have to learn everything about each other's bodies to enjoy sex, but you do have to learn how to keep your ego in check and how to not bring your mental projections and desires onto an arena that is so pure, so divine, so transcendental.

Your mind has no business in sex. Even your body has no business - but there is no other way. Initially, you need the body but after a while, even your body should become secondary. You both should be lost somewhere in an internal space that you cannot even understand. You should forget where you are. You should forget what you're doing. Your entire awareness should be on the inside, not on the outside. First, you need to drop the mind, and then you need to drop the body, and then the merger happens.

THE SOUL OF SEXUALITY

What is the connection between spirituality, sex, and gender? Does spirituality affect my sexual desires or preferences?

Let's attempt to define the word "spirituality." There is a lot of misconception surrounding it. Firstly, spirituality is not magic, voodoo, or merely a way of defining things. It is not a strange way of life. Spirituality is simply a quest to know yourself. The reason for delaying the search for a spiritual way of life is simply that you don't know who you are. You are grappling with the strangeness of life, the mind, and the body, and trying to find yourself amidst these forces. If you knew exactly who you are, what your purpose is, and what you're meant to be, then your quality of life would be totally different. You would not be plagued by problems, worries about your looks, or troubled by your self-identity. You would not be agitated by what's happening internally or externally. The very fact that your life is disrupted indicates that there is a vast unknown that needs addressing. Spirituality is a way of addressing that. It is the oldest system, method, and process of self-inquiry, of diving into the depths of your being, of asking the right questions, and of exercising that fundamental curiosity to know, not just about what's happening externally, but most importantly, about yourself.

Who am I?

At the heart of spirituality lies the question: Who am I? Not just as a body or a mind, but existentially, who am I? The moment you answer that question, everything else will fall into place. Without answering it, you will never fully settle with yourself. There's a profound connection between spirituality, sex, and gender. If spirituality is a search for yourself, then because you don't know who you are, you're searching for yourself amidst uncertainty about two fundamental processes: sex and your self-identity, which is sometimes referred to as gender. "I'm a man," "I'm a woman," or "I'm something else." Without understanding the connection between spirituality and sex, it's impossible to comprehend gender.

One of the biggest problems in modern society is that we're trying to define gender without considering spirituality. We're neglecting the fundamental understanding that we're all in a state of flux, constantly searching for ourselves. Self-identity isn't fixed; we grapple with the question of who we are every moment. However, there's a strange phenomenon emerging where the disconnection between the mind and the body is becoming so pronounced that some individuals feel they've been placed in the wrong body. It's an extreme expression of dissatisfaction with one's body. Almost eighty percent of Americans don't like their bodies and spend their lives struggling to connect with them, either through cosmetic alterations or milder physical changes like exercise, all in pursuit of an ideal appearance. Deeper still, some individuals resort to extreme measures, seeking to drastically alter their bodies to erase their basic physical identity.

For example, there's a man, the kind you'd see as healthy and good-looking by our usual standards of beauty. At some point, this notion crept into his mind that he's not human; he's actually an alien. He's not merely saying, "I like aliens. I'm into the whole idea of aliens." No, it's deeper than that. He's taken this fondness, this ongoing conversation in his head about aliens, to such an extreme that he's completely forgotten his human identity. He's fully embraced the notion of being an alien to the extent that he's even altering his physical appearance to resemble one. Now, who's to say what an alien looks like? It's purely a product of our imagination. The alien images we conjure up are essentially our simplistic way of envisioning something different from ourselves. They still have to bear some resemblance to us because if they're too far off, we can't relate. So, they need to be familiar yet different enough to captivate us and catch our interest because they're something new.

So, this alien, in our minds, has a head, but it's larger. It's got eyes, but they're bigger, and a nose, maybe even smaller, sometimes barely there. Ears? Sure, but they're massive. And instead of five fingers, perhaps just three. This is all just our imagination at play. But then, he began to truly believe that this is who he is. He embarked on what he called the "Black Alien Project," covering his entire body in permanent black tattoos. Every inch. Then came the surgeries. First, his nose, then his lips, then his ears. He even had two fingers removed from each hand. If you were to see him now, it would be a challenge to recognize him as human. Sure, he's got the general form, but his appearance and mannerisms all echo this imaginary idea of an alien.

This is a perfect example to show how far you can stretch the disconnect between your mind and body. If you don't know how to listen to your body, if you have forgotten how to listen to your body, if your mind has become your only reality, if the conversation in your head is the only thing you know, then what happens if that conversation starts contradicting the body? What if, in your conversations, you start seeing yourself as something other than what your body is so openly showing? If you want to know whether you are male or female, stand in front of the mirror.

There are cases, however, where there is a disconnection between the hormones and the body. That's a different matter altogether. I'm talking about people with normal body functions and normal heart functions. They can see in the mirror that their body is of a particular sex - male or female, but in their mind, they have created such a big divide. They hate the body so much that they begin to think they are stuck in the wrong body.

It's the same discomfort, the same disconnect we have with the body, taken to an extreme. I am not saying that there aren't individuals who simply don't identify with who they are on the outside. There could be such an extreme case where, right from the beginning, right from their childhood, their identity was shaped differently, but even in those cases, if you are given a choice to listen to your mind or your body, you have to choose to listen to your body. Barring a few exceptional cases, most scenarios where an individual is saying that they are stuck in the wrong body are simply echoing the same thing people have been saying for a long time: They don't connect with the body. They're not getting the love, they're not getting the appreciation. It's basically that they want to be something other than what they are, which is a very common thought - a thought that crosses a normal mind all the time: "I don't like my life; I don't like my nose; I don't like my hair." That is why we see people putting so much emphasis on how they look, so much emphasis on trying to alter their looks.

Now, when that is taken to an extreme, we might want to alter our sex. In most cases, it is an extreme psychological problem, not a physical one. Because the problem is not addressed, because individuals have not been given a tool, a method, or a way to self-inquire, understand more about themselves, and connect more with their minds and bodies, they eventually reach a point where they are unable to stand their bodies. In my opinion, if an individual has reached a point where they are unable to accept their body and want to change it completely, they have reached a suicidal point. Whatever they do after that to try and alter their body - because they're unable to end their life completely, because they're not able to kill themselves fully - they are killing themselves slowly. There's no way a body that is perfectly designed to be a man can be perfectly turned into a woman, or vice-versa. You can try, but you will fail.

GLOBAL WEIRDING

Look at the irony of this: an individual wants to change their body because people are not accepting them for who they are, "Because people are looking at me as someone else; they are not seeing who I am." Now, here you are wanting the whole world to accept you, and you cannot accept your own body. How can you expect the world to accept you, to love you, when you don't love your own body? To cover this up, we talk about rights, we talk about being open enough to accept all kinds of people. Yes, we have to be open to accepting all kinds of people. But you have to draw the line somewhere as a society. If you can't tell someone, "You are acting stupid," then you are neither helping them nor helping yourself. You are saying, "I don't care. I don't care what happens to people. I don't care whether individuals ruin themselves."

Most of these people who have issues with connecting with their bodies and take this to the extreme are young people between the ages of thirteen to twenty-five. Now, as a society, those who have lived longer, those who have lived before them, if they are unable to look at these people and say, "There's something wrong with you; let me help you. Let me help you reconnect with your body. Let me help you to re-understand life," then it's as good as saying that we will accept all kinds of weirdness.

Thomas Friedman, in his book discussing global warming, says it's not just about global warming. The changing weather patterns and the evolving landscape of climate will eventually lead to what is called "global weirding," where some places will get hotter and others cooler. There will be various weather irregularities. So, he coined the term "global weirding." What we are experiencing in the sexual sphere, in the sphere of self-identity, is a form of global weirding to the point where we are unable to understand the simple difference between the mind and the body. Your mind is always whimsical; it is an entity that cannot be trusted. If your mind tells you that you are stuck in the wrong body and you listen to that, you are being foolish.

The work has to be done on the mind, not on the body - not for anybody else's sake, but for your own. It is easier to alter the mind than the body, while it appears like it's easy to just change your body. You don't have to go into meditation, meditatively understand what's happening in your mind, reconcile your past, or look at what has happened to you. You can simply put your body under the knife and remove those parts that you don't like. That seems like a simple, straightforward solution. But it isn't. You cannot alter the body from the outside.

NO GENDER

The body and self-identity go deep, but you can alter your mind. You can alter the conversation in your head. If you have conditioned yourself to believe that you are a man or a woman, you can also decondition yourself. Now, why is this possible? Firstly, deep down inside, we are neither male nor female. That is the whole essence of spirituality - to get to a point where you simply connect to your true self, which is independent of your gender, independent of your body, independent of your mind, just a pure being.

Just like when you look at a tree: a tree is neither male nor female, but it is still there. It is still alive. It is still fruiting, and flowering. You don't exclusively recognize a tree as male or female. There are trees with both male and female parts, some trees which can be recognized as male, and some which can be recognized as female. This is only when you dig deeper. When you look at it from the outside, it is just an expression of life. So is the human body. It is we humans who are totally obsessed with gender, obsessed with recognizing ourselves as being male or female. What we are given is a body. We don't have a choice. You are you, either way. And most importantly, you are an entity that is independent of the mind and the body. You are simply using the mind and the body. You're playing with the body. You're playing with the mind, and therein lies your happiness. That is where you find your joy. You did not overly attach yourself to the body or the mind. But what happens as you start growing up, as your body becomes more and more recognizable to people around you - your identity is solidified. Your name, the clothes you wear, your hairstyle, the bathroom you use, the way people identify you, which box you check - male or female - all these things put together become your identity and your gender identity.

Now, where is this coming from? It's actually coming from the body and the recognition of the body by people around us. Now, imagine if you were living on an island, all alone. No other human beings. Would you ever ask this question: Am I a man or a woman? That question would never arise in your mind. Now, can you survive without that question? Absolutely. Can you sing without that question? Yes. Can you dance without that question? Yes. You can breathe, you can digest your food, you can reproduce, you can do everything without ever worrying about that question.

When you are alone, it just doesn't matter. Once we understand that our identity actually comes from people, from the world we live in, we see the implications of trying to alter that identity. If you attempt to convince the whole world to see you differently, you will be spending the rest of your life torturing your body and mind. Eventually, you will die a lonely, disappointed individual.

This might seem very harsh. Again, I'm not saying that there are no individuals who cannot identify with their bodies. There are extreme cases. But generally, for most of us, this disconnect is simply in our minds. We don't like the body. We don't like the world. We don't like how people look at us. We take that animosity against the body and the world to an extreme. What we should be doing, in fact, is trying to connect with that part of us that knows neither male nor female. And if you look at ancient scriptures, there's a clear mention of this. If you are a man before awakening, you must pass through the feminine aspect. If you are a woman before becoming awakened, enlightened, you must pass through the masculine. So, what are 'man' and 'woman?' These are qualities, not fixed entities. Certain qualities can be recognized as masculine and others as feminine. Throughout the day, you shift between these identities. Sometimes you identify with the masculine qualities, sometimes with the feminine. But the moment you start rejecting one in favor of the other, aided by your imagination, you are creating the perfect conditions for imbalance - an imbalance that can lead to all kinds of extremes.

The function of the imagination is not so much to make strange things settle, as it is to make settled things strange. Friedman is right; that's what imagination does. Its job is to stir things up and even take those things that are settled and turn them unsettled. You have a body with a settled identity, with settled biological and hormonal processes. Now, you are using your imagination to alter it. And you're hiding all this behind one line: "I am stuck in a different body spiritually." If you understand that your identity cannot be separate from your body, then whatever identity you recognize as something separate from your body is neither male nor female. So the moment you say, "I am a woman inside a man's body," you have misunderstood imagination for reality. You have turned a conversation into a truth for yourself.

There are moments when my mind says, "I wish I was a woman." I connect with women more. I mean, I've said this several times. As a spiritual person, I understand women more, but that doesn't mean I am a woman. That doesn't mean I dislike the idea of being a man. Despite my frequent criticism of men, if you were to just listen to my criticism, you might think that I hate my body or hate being a man - not at all. I know where my criticism is coming from. It originates from my mind, from what I'm observing. I know why I'm criticizing and understand the difference between who I am and what I'm saying. There should be a difference because who you are has nothing to do with whether you identify yourself as a man or a woman - who you are is something different. I unconditionally love my body. I connect with women. I connect with feminine qualities, but I am a man. That is my identity. Can I change that identity? Yes, I can. But I would be wasting so much energy trying to convince someone else.

Ultimately, I would only change my body to convince others or myself. But really, I just need to feel right on the inside. Whether I'm seen as a man or a woman outside doesn't matter. It's only when I seek acceptance from the world that I feel pushed to change my body. You could spend your whole life trying to show others who you are, but it's a waste because it's impossible for anyone to truly see your inner self. People don't see you for who you are; they see what they want to see. Again, when we say "people," are we talking about the entire human race? Would you be able to convince the entire human race that you are a man or a woman? What if there's one individual whom you are unable to convince? Would you go and try to convince them? Would you alter yourself even more?

There's no end to this - trying to satisfy the world, trying to satisfy the people around us, and trying to alter our insides and outsides to fit in the eyes of the world is a futile attempt. This is where spirituality comes into the picture. Spirituality understands that there is a conflict inside. We are all born with conflict, we grow up in conflict, and society adds to that conflict. The conflict is mostly a misunderstanding of words. Experientially, these things don't matter to us at all. Think about it: a food that tastes good to a man tastes equally good to a woman. The food does not make any distinction. An apple tastes pretty much the same for both a man and a woman. Almost all things are like this. Existence does not make any distinctions. It is willing to bestow its gifts on you irrespective of who you are or what you identify with.

That should tell us that firstly, we should not encourage or push our society in the direction of attaching ourselves too much to the idea of male and female. We should be cautious about centering all our discussions around gender and sex because we are missing something more important. We are failing to ask more fundamental questions. The question is not whether you are a man or a woman; the question is, who are you?

Eventually, both the man and the woman have to be transcended. That is what spirituality is about - going beyond these identities to become a pure being, going beyond all the words, and understanding where the misunderstandings originate. We are creating more and more words, more and more differentiation. We are frustrated that people are not understanding these differentiations. For example, coming from India, I might not have heard many of these terminologies. In fact, it was only after coming to America that I began to explore the definition of acronyms - what does LGBTQ mean? But by the time I began to understand what LGBTQ is, three more letters were added to it.

Now, it's not that experientially, I don't understand what these are, but you cannot expect me to exactly understand what these words mean because these words are constantly being defined and redefined. It's a very fluid space. But ignorance of the actual meaning of these words cannot be equated with ignorance in people. That does not mean that people are not open-minded. Just because someone is unable to identify you with the gender you have identified with, doesn't mean they are not open-minded. It doesn't mean they don't love or care. It could just be that they don't understand. Some things are a little difficult to understand, and it might take a little longer.

The direction in which we should be moving is clear: we should love people whether we understand them or not. Love should be the foundation. Then, we can talk about our differences. Yes, I may disagree with your decision to alter your gender on the outside, to put your body through that ordeal, but that doesn't mean that I don't love you. As a person, as an individual, you deserve love. Each and every individual deserves love, even if their actions seem misguided on the outside. The only way we can reach that place is to accept that there is no connection between love and understanding. Understanding is an ongoing process. It is a lifelong journey, but love is existential. You don't become more loving over time. You are love. You are an expression of love, and you must connect with people through love at the most fundamental level, whether you understand them or not.

A passage from "Sex at Dawn" comes to mind.

It was early spring 1519. Hernan Cortez and his men had just arrived off the coast of the Mexican mainland. The conquistador ordered his men to bring one of the natives to the deck of the ship where Cortez asked him the name of this exotic place they had found. The man responded, "Ma c'ubah than," which the Spanish heard as "Yucatan."

Close enough. Cortez proclaimed that from that day onward Yucatan and any gold it contained belonged to Spain and so on. Four and a half centuries later in the 1970s, linguists researching archaic Mayan dialects concluded that "Ma c'ubah than" meant "I do not understand you."

Let us accept that we don't understand each other because we are trying to understand our own invention - words - and we have to pour meaning into these words. We have to define them. There will be misunderstandings. There is no need to hate each other just because we are unable to understand each other.

That is what spirituality is. Spirituality takes you to a space where you become love itself, where you can accept the differences of people. You can openly speak your mind without having to worry about criticism and judgment, as long as you believe in and understand the value of what you're sharing, and the value of how you are recognizing another individual. The moment you know that your criticism is coming from a place of love - even what appears to be your anger or frustration, if it is coming from a space of love, it means you are angry and frustrated about what's happening on the outside because you love people, because you care about humanity. That is what spirituality does. It connects you to yourself. It connects you to that deeper realm of aliveness within you so that you can embody it and connect with everything around you through love. Love can accommodate all things, all differences, and all misunderstandings.

SELF-PLEASURE

How can masturbation be used as a tool for enlightenment?

I like the question. You're not asking *if* masturbation can be used as a tool for enlightenment, but rather *how* it can be. This recognizes that masturbation isn't inherently evil or something to be shunned. Historically, society - often influenced by religious views - has stigmatized masturbation. To find a cultural acceptance of masturbation, one might look as far back as ancient Egyptian civilization, where it was depicted in statues. Similarly, ancient Rome recognized masturbation as a natural form of self-pleasure. However, the Hebrew Old Testament opposed all sexual behaviors outside of heterosexual marriage, leading to the condemnation of masturbation, among other acts.

The term "masturbation" is believed to originate from the Latin "manstuprare," a combination of "manus" (hand) and "stuprare" (to defile or to sexually pollute), highlighting a deep-seated misunderstanding. Even the word itself suggests using one's hand to tarnish one's sexuality.

Nonetheless, scientific understanding has thoroughly debunked the notion that masturbation is detrimental. It is not only beneficial but incredibly healthy. The process of masturbation - from engaging the mind and stimulating the body to touching pleasure centers and reaching orgasm - provides substantial health benefits on mental, physical, and spiritual levels.

WHY MASTURBATE?

Masturbation in itself is not wrong, but it's worth exploring why we feel the need to engage in it. Why do we resort to masturbation? Firstly, it's clear there is nothing inherently negative about it, and it is extraordinarily common. Nearly ninety to ninety-five percent of people around the world are familiar with masturbation, and most have engaged in it at least once. If they've done it once, they've likely done it many times. There's also a significant misconception that frequent masturbation, particularly among men, is problematic. Many men approach this topic with great uncertainty and fear, as if something is wrong. For example, some might ask, "I masturbate two to three times a day, every day. Is this wrong?" The answer is no. The body is perfectly capable of handling multiple sessions of masturbation in a day. The only negative aspect arises when it becomes so frequent that it starts to interfere with personal and social life. Imagine avoiding work because you want to stay home and masturbate, or masturbating to the point of exhaustion. These are extreme cases where masturbation might be impacting your life negatively.

Masturbating multiple times a day generally has no adverse effects on your health, either physical or mental. But is it natural? Do we see masturbation in nature as commonly as we see it in human societies? No, we don't. Animals don't masturbate nearly as much as human beings, largely because they live in environments where there are no restrictions on expressing their sexuality. Their lives are arranged and organized in such a way that a partner is always available, or their bodily and metabolic changes during off-seasons mean they aren't even thinking about sex. Most animals are not constantly sexual; they experience heightened sexuality only during certain periods.

We humans, on the other hand, have created artificial barriers for ourselves. We have constructed societal norms and structures that obstruct the free expression and movement of our sexuality. Since the desire to find pleasure in sex is such a strong force, we resort to masturbation. There's nothing inherently wrong with masturbation, but if there is a way to create conditions that allow your natural sexuality to express itself and find its avenue, that should be preferred over masturbation.

Now, why did this happen? What led to curbing our sexual activities using our own systems and processes? We created these rules and restrictions ourselves; no other species imposed them on us. Firstly, it was due to a misunderstanding of what sex is. Even now, the standard dictionary definition of sex implies a normal heterosexual relationship where penetration is involved. If there is no penetration, it is not recognized as sex. Thus, all types of sex are categorized primarily based on where penetration occurs. However, if you think about it, pleasure has nothing to do with penetration. Orgasm has nothing to do with penetration. In fact, we could use a completely different word to describe pleasure. You could call it an orgasm, which has nothing to do with sex.

Once you understand that sex and orgasm are two completely different things, you realize that sex is a necessity only for reproduction. It is not necessary for experiencing an orgasm or for pleasure. Because we failed to make this separation, because we saw sex and pleasure as one, and because we had already regarded sex as something that must be preserved and conserved, consider this: Every time a man masturbates and ejaculates, you might think he's squandering potential future children. Approaching it with that idea naturally leads to opposition against masturbation. You are seen as wasting your life energies. This is where all the ideas connected to masturbation come from. Why it is viewed as evil, and why it is seen as unnatural? Because there is no reproduction happening, the other partner is missing, and you are using sex purely for pleasure when, in fact, sex has been exclusively dedicated to reproduction.

If you go back in time, you'll see that it was normal for both men and women to produce as many children as possible. There was no concept of controlling childbirth. Once two individuals were married, a woman was almost always pregnant or raising children. This consumed most of her time, leaving her little opportunity to even think about masturbation; she was too busy raising her children. We know how much energy, time, and physical involvement it takes to raise children. In a way, women didn't talk about or assert their right to masturbate because they were married off so early and became mothers so quickly. They identified primarily as mothers and did not see themselves as individuals who deserved their own personal space and happiness. For a man, sex was always available, regardless of whether or not the woman wanted it.

When he wanted to have sex, he did, and the woman simply had to consent.

This unnatural environment and social structure suppressed the need to masturbate, fostering the misunderstanding that your body is organized solely around the reproductive system. However, for both males and females, there is a completely different channel that runs through the body, dedicated solely to pleasure. When you observe the same body parts from one dimension, they appear entirely geared towards reproduction. Biologically, it's easy to see how every part assists in creating babies. Yet, if you view it from the perspective of the individual - from that space where someone is seeking release, looking for a way to transcend the stress and strain of the body, and aiming to experience a moment of deep bliss or orgasm - you will see that every part of the body is perfectly designed to aid in the process of finding pleasure internally.

The entire human mechanism can be understood independently, based solely on its design for experiencing pleasure. However, because we analyzed life solely from an external, religious perspective - distant from individual, bodily experiences - we failed to acknowledge that humans are inherently pleasure-seeking. There is something within us that constantly seeks release, regardless of whether we have children, whether we are married, or whether we are already getting enough sex. It has nothing to do with external circumstances; it is an internal mechanism. Due to our failure to understand this aspect, we did not create a social structure that supports this natural expression of pleasure. As a result, human beings eventually had to resort to masturbation.

There is no way to address this issue other than by fundamentally reevaluating how we live, where we live, and whom we live with. As long as we are isolated, living alone or just one man and one woman together, the only ways to connect with the deeper layers of yourself are through masturbation. Setting aside meditation and spirituality, the only way to fully explore the possibilities of your sexuality is to discover it for yourself. Your body is perfectly capable of providing this experience. However, if we want to explore ourselves naturally with the help of partners, then we must reconsider our societal structure and reorganize it around community living.

This can happen at the family level. Individuals can come together; a few families can unite to embrace a communal way of living. This might seem like a regression since we originated from communal living, moved to cities, and then became isolated. But now we can see that the only way to grant human sexuality its freedom is to facilitate access to people, starting with families, friends, relatives, and people we know, by revisiting the idea of communal living. Almost every place that identifies as a community, whether it be a church, a club, or any gathering spot, shares something. This shared aspect can foster deeper connections and allow for a more natural expression of human sexuality within a supportive communal framework.

We need to reconsider the restrictions we have placed on sex. These places could become wonderful avenues for people to connect with each other and to express their sexuality naturally. However, we are very far from reimagining society in this way. We have drifted so far into isolated living and have become so invested in the idea of marriage that the notion of a chess club or a church as places where one might also engage in sexual activities seems absurd. Yet, if we truly want to free human beings, help them connect with themselves, and become more spiritual and natural, this is the path we should consider. Wherever there is an opportunity for people to come together, there should also be an opportunity for them to openly express their sexuality.

Viewed from the current societal perspective, this idea seems ridiculous and disruptive. It might appear that it would lead people to become overly focused on sex, discussing and thinking about nothing else. What then would be the purpose of a church if it were also a place for sexual encounters? Such questions arise because we are looking at this from a repressed state. To move forward, we must shift our perspective and consider more open expressions of human sexuality as natural and healthy integrations into our social spaces. When society is liberated in this manner, the stigma and repression associated with sex will diminish. Then, these places won't become perverted spaces where individuals are only looking for sex because, with such openness, the obsessive desire for sex is likely to decrease. This accessibility shifts focus from mere pursuit of pleasure to meaningful engagement.

Consider this: in masturbation, unless you know what you're doing and have ample time, the interaction is brief. You're not fully engaged, and the lesser the involvement, the less likely the act can be seen as a pathway to something deeper or spiritual. However, when you have a partner, when there are no restrictions, when you're living in a community where sex is open and available, you're more likely to explore and take your time. In such a context, if the idea is introduced that sex can be a pathway to awakening or enlightenment, people will begin to see and experience this naturally. This shift in perception enables a deeper exploration of sexuality as not just a physical act, but a significant component of our spiritual and personal development.

Awakening Through Masturbation

Because sex is now viewed as unnatural, the idea that it can be spiritual also seems unnatural. The same goes for masturbation. Since it is still regarded as something wrong, it is done in private, secretly, and often hurriedly. As a result, it's difficult to see how masturbation could lead to enlightenment or awakening. Yet, masturbation could potentially lead to awakening more directly, with less confusion and frustration, because it involves only the individual. You only need to learn about your own body without the complexities of teaching someone else or worrying about their cooperation. The body is perfectly conducive to this. It is designed to aid in using sex and masturbation as tools for transcendence and awakening.

To illustrate why we struggle to naturally express our sexuality despite having all the necessary resources - intelligence, physicality, and community - consider this: We live in an era of abundance. Existence, by nature, is abundant, especially concerning matters of sex, where there is no inherent scarcity. Yet, we find ourselves competing for sexual experiences. We exert effort, apply our creativity, pursue education, and seek better jobs, all with the underlying belief that these will enhance our sexual experiences. Society perpetuates the notion that greater wealth and success lead to better sex.

This framework of competition for what should be a natural and abundant aspect of life creates a kind of poverty - a poverty of genuine sexual expression, which, like all forms of poverty, is man-made. This illustrates how societal structures and cultural attitudes can distort natural human instincts and create unnecessary struggles for fulfillment.

You're not living in a realm of scarcity. Existence isn't denying you anything; everything is available. Just as malnutrition is often a direct result of political structures that prevent people from living naturally, our quest for sex, our struggle for it, and the barriers we encounter are all of our own making. We have created an artificial structure that conditions us to believe that sex is not easy to obtain, and that you must work hard for it.

Consider a study that was conducted to show changes in animal behavior when placed in environments that mirror how humans live. This study, using chimpanzees, illustrates how even animals can exhibit unnatural behaviors when subjected to human-like constraints, further highlighting how our social and environmental conditions shape our perceptions and actions, particularly regarding natural impulses like sexuality.

Initially, when the chimps were introduced to the room with abundant food, they behaved as they do in the wild. In their natural habitat, when a chimp finds a fruit tree, it doesn't immediately start eating. Instead, it calls over its family members and group to share the discovery. This behavior is rooted in the natural abundance of their environment - when one chimp finds a fruit-laden tree, they all share. This collaborative and sharing behavior highlights the instinct of sharing that arises in environments of plenty.

Initially, the experiment with the chimps replicated their natural behaviors: when food was abundant, they called others to share, just as they would in the wild. However, as researchers gradually reduced the quantity of food to a limited amount, the chimps' behavior changed dramatically. Initially, they stopped calling others when they found food and began to eat immediately. As food became scarcer, their behavior became aggressive; they started pushing other chimps aside.

These chimps, biologically predisposed to cooperation and social living, shifted to a survival mode that prioritized individual needs over group survival. Their behavior mirrored human actions - fighting and competing - highlighting a fundamental change brought on by scarcity.

This scenario is a stark reflection of human society. Naturally, humans are cooperative; we thrive in social groups and share communal experiences, including sex. We are inherently social beings. However, the current societal structure promotes isolation and individualism, where self-interest and personal gain are prioritized. Families and individuals focus on accumulating wealth for themselves, often at the expense of broader social connections. Society has become a competitive place, a stark contrast to our natural inclinations towards community and sharing. This shift underscores the profound impact of environmental and societal conditions on behavior, both in chimps and humans.

We have moved humanity into a very unnatural environment, one that fundamentally alters their basic way of living. Now we complain about humans being greedy, not sharing, and being selfish, but these conditions were created by the very structure of our society. We have imposed the most significant restrictions on one of the most enjoyable aspects of human life: sex. By not allowing free and natural expression of sexuality, we've prompted people to view each other as competitors.

It's basic psychology that when denied something, people often project their frustrations onto others. This mindset, "I am not getting it because you are also competing for it," is where many ideas of competition originate. This perspective is also why we fear an expanding population. Instead of celebrating the growth and multiplication of human beings, we dread it because we don't like each other. This sentiment is rooted deeply in our minds: more people means more resources are needed, which implies less for me. We fear that we will need to cut down more forests and kill more animals.

This is a completely unnatural way of thinking. We have turned against our own kind and are unable to accept the natural part of human existence, which is to multiply and grow. Why? Because we are not living in a natural environment. We have been conditioned to believe that the things we most desire are not available in abundance and that these are the things we need to strive for and work towards.

THE CLITORAL NETWORK

As long as we are living in such an environment, our options are limited, leading us to turn to masturbation. If we assume there is no hope for changing the social system, there remains hope in the idea that masturbation alone can facilitate enlightenment; masturbation alone is sufficient for awakening. Our understanding should begin with separating sex from pleasure, and it's easier to start with females because they possess a special organ dedicated solely to pleasure, unrelated to reproduction or the elimination of bodily waste. This organ is the clitoris, which is not just a small dot; it is a complete organ. Just as a male's penis extends outward, a female's clitoris extends inward. In fact, it is said that the male penis is essentially an inverted clitoris. You can compare the male penis to the female clitoris to see that it has all the corresponding parts, only most of the clitoris is hidden inside, while for a man, it's on the outside.

Here's a surprising fact: almost all mammals have a clitoris, indicating that the ability to connect with a pleasure center independent of reproduction exists naturally in nature. It's a fascinating thought - what if animals were introduced to their clitoris? What would they do? Leaving that aside, let's return to our human species. Pleasure need not be connected with sex, a concept we often define as involving penetration. Here lies an organ specifically designed to provide female pleasure independently of penetration: the clitoris. It's important to understand a few things about this organ, highlighted by a passage from Natalie Angier, who speaks eloquently about the clitoral network:

"Nerves are like wolves or birds. If one starts crying, there goes the neighborhood." This encourages us to rethink the clitoris not as a mere bump but as a complex network, a pleasure dome, the Xanadu at the heart of female sexuality, because it is all that and more.

When engorged with blood during sexual arousal, the clitoris increases in size, much like a penis. In fact, both the clitoris and the penis originate from the same embryonic tissue and can be compared point by point. However, unlike the penis, which is burdened with the responsibilities of reproduction and waste removal, the clitoris is devoted solely to pleasure. This devotion grants women an infinitely greater capacity for sexual response than men can ever dream of."

Ms. Angier beautifully points out that the organ dedicated to pleasure is there for us to understand and utilize. But how do we do this effectively? Understanding masturbation isn't overly complex - there's a natural rhythm to seeking pleasure, and through exploration, one can discover the pleasure centers. However, the real question is: How do you transform this experience into something spiritually profound? How do you turn mere pleasure into bliss?

The key distinction here is that while pleasure is momentary, bliss is enduring. For something to qualify as bliss, it should be something you can experience for an extended period, not just fleetingly or in bursts, but with continuity.

There is a method to approach masturbation that involves slowly and gradually increasing your awareness, using your breath, and being mindful of body sensations. By doing so, you can connect multiple orgasms, stringing them together into one cohesive and complete experience. This is what we seek in the pursuit of awakening or enlightenment.

The crucial factor is awareness - what are you focusing on during masturbation? Are you simply watching a sex video, or are you thinking about a celebrity crush? Or, more importantly, are you attuned to the sensations themselves? This focus is crucial. Often, we get caught up in visualizations or fantasies during the pleasure-seeking process, influenced by our fascination with sex and our partners' bodies. However, the true transformative potential lies in focusing on the physical sensations themselves, moving beyond mere fantasy to a deeper, more introspective experience.

Spirituality begins to diverge from mere physical stimulation at this point. You continue to stimulate and touch your pleasure centers, but the challenge is to gradually reduce your reliance on visual images or the idea of another body. Instead, try to connect directly with your pleasure center. This deeper connection is only feasible when you dedicate adequate time to masturbation. If you're seeking quick pleasure, yes, five to ten minutes might suffice. However, if your goal is to transform this activity into a spiritual practice, you should consider extending the duration to thirty minutes, an hour, or possibly even longer. It doesn't have to be as frequent, but it should be more profound when it does occur.

This approach is applicable to both men and women. A man can also use masturbation as a pathway to awakening, though his journey might be more complex. After reaching climax, a man typically experiences a refractory period where he cannot continue immediately. Therefore, his approach must be more gradual. He cannot rush directly to the pleasure center because the moment he reaches it, he's temporarily ousted from that state. For a man, the technique must involve a blend of silence and stillness. Traditional meditation can greatly assist in this process. By going deeper into meditation, a man can better connect with the pleasure center and maintain that connection for a longer duration, transforming the experience into one of sustained spiritual and sensual engagement.

For women, the journey to spiritual awakening through masturbation may not necessarily require traditional meditation, and this accessibility could be one reason why spiritual communities have historically hesitated to admit women. The fear might have stemmed from the recognition that it's a more straightforward process for women, who can revisit their pleasure center repeatedly with relative ease. With a bit of understanding, the use of mindful awareness, and proper breathing techniques, women can potentially reach enlightenment more quickly and with greater pleasure.

The process for women involves recognizing that deeper states of bliss - states beyond our normal comprehension - are indeed attainable. These states, which enlightened beings like Buddha described as "awakening," "the profound experience of self-realization," are accessible through orgasm and masturbation. To tap into this potential, one must approach the practice spiritually and consciously, with a slow and deliberate focus, and with an awareness that such experiences are not only possible but transformative. This method underscores a spiritual dimension to pleasure that transcends conventional physical satisfaction, offering a pathway to profound personal insight and enlightenment.

I leave you with one woman's description of touching this deeper zone, and she did it just through masturbation - the literal definition of the word using her own hands. She polluted herself to enlightenment. This is Keeley Olivia's description of her experience of masturbation:

"About forty minutes into my self-pleasure practice, something remarkable took place. A supernova happened in my vagina. I'm sure at that moment, my vagina was the brightest shining object in all of our galaxy. The eruption began from deep within my soul and pleasure previously unknown to me cascaded from the center of my being and rippled out to the tips of my body which should merge with the corners of the ever-expanding universe. I became all of time and space. Eternal benevolent blackness enveloped me interconnecting me to everything all at once. Pure, present consciousness. Not a thought or worry existed. It seemed to last forever. Me floating between worlds. Traveling through space on this giant marshmallow of cosmic angelic pleasure. And then this miraculous cackle penetrated my awareness from somewhere in the distance and I realized it had traversed out of my own mouth and emanated from the most ancient part of my womb, and I was back in the room

and tears were streaming down my face. Tears of joy. Tears of gratitude. Tears of enchantment, wonder, and awe. I had danced with grace through my vagina, through my cervix, the actual gateway which opens when every human life is ready to enter the physical from the mystical."

Orgasm

TOGETHER IN SPIRIT

What is your opinion on same-sex couples? Can couples of the same sex help each other grow spiritually?

There is a lot of misunderstanding when it comes to accepting the idea of same-sex couples and their attraction towards each other and their choices. Now, where does this misunderstanding come from? Firstly, we, as a society, have accepted certain arbitrary rules about what is normal and what is not. In fact, we ourselves have no clear idea of what "normal" is. We keep changing this idea of "normal," adapting it to suit our requirements. For example, one common argument against any sexual orientation other than what is recognized as normal - attraction of males towards females and females towards males - is regarded as unnatural. Critics argue, "We don't see it in nature. It is a perversion. Something has gone wrong." However, there is ample evidence in nature, among animals, that sexual differences are not as defined as they appear to be. This occurs because we cling to a clear demarcation between males and females.

WHAT IS "NATURAL"

For us, sex is typically between opposite sexes. We look for the same patterns when we study animals, often focusing on those that are closer to us in form, movement, and actions. We're also looking for behaviors that are familiar to us. However, the animal kingdom is filled with examples of individuals exhibiting all kinds of orientations. Take bonobos, for instance. These apes, which are biologically very closely related to humans, engage in behaviors where almost sixty percent of sexual activities occur between two female bonobos. These interactions do not result in reproduction; rather, they are part of their social behavior. Yet, how often do we hear about these examples? Not only is sexual preference individualistic but also the physical distinctions between male and female are not as clear-cut as we might think.

For example, consider honey bees. If you study their reproduction process, you'll be amazed to find that bees reproduce in an entirely different way than humans. It's not simply one male and one female mating to produce offspring. Instead, there's one queen bee, and once she is fertilized by several males, she is capable of laying thousands of eggs. When she lays the egg, she can produce males (drones) or females (workers). Drones are created when she chooses not to fertilize; when she fertilizes, workers are produced. What you see in a bee colony are mostly workers because drones do not work; they are produced solely for mating and then they die.

There are innumerable examples in our oceans where it is difficult to even recognize the differences between males and females. Some creatures change sex within their lifetime, depending on conditions, like crocodiles. The sex of baby crocodiles is not determined by the parents but by the temperature of the environment. Depending on the temperature, either the entire clutch will be male or female.

What we recognize as a fundamental differentiation at the genetic level that seems unalterable, the animal kingdom presents plenty of examples to show that the differentiation we identify as sexual - as male or female - is not as distinct as it appears. Moreover, there is a whole spectrum of what we recognize as sexes in between male and female.

What we are observing now, in terms of identifying individuals with different sexual orientations, is only possible due to the connectivity of the modern generation. We can see more of what's happening in the world and hear differing opinions. We are moving towards a more individualistic society, which is why we are getting to know about individual preferences that we normally wouldn't hear about. There was a time when the so-called majority, brainwashed and conditioned by religions that condemned anything other than what they recognized as normal, hardly heard about individual experiences of sexual orientations that deviated from the norm. Any sign that an individual was deviating from the recognized norm meant immediate punishment; they were burned at the stake. Consequently, nobody dared to acknowledge a different sexual orientation. It was there, but remained unspoken and suffered in silence.

There is no doubt that our desire to connect with another human being is more vibrant and varied than we can possibly imagine. This is not solely the making of the mind; individuals are born with certain tendencies and grow up with them. If such possibilities did not exist in nature or human communities - if gays and lesbians were merely imagining themselves to be such - then we would not see examples where individual bodies cannot be clearly defined as male or female.

Again, we can find all kinds of examples because we know that form is influenced by multiple factors. It is influenced by our orientation, which is essentially the way we think, the kinds of thoughts we entertain, and the desires we have. Then there is the body itself: biologically, was it meant to be male or female? And then some hormones define how much a male is male and how much a female is female. These are all fluid, changing processes; they are not as fixed as they appear to be.

Individual Preferences

Now, why is there so much misunderstanding when it comes to accepting same-sex couples? It's because, by nature, sexes and preferences are an acquired taste. There is nothing universal about the preferences of individuals. There's nothing standard, nothing fixed. It is an acquired taste. Your mind is involved in the process. That is why preferences, even among same-sex couples, are very specific and narrow.

Of all the individuals, consider a woman who is attracted to a man, but not to every man. She has a very narrow band of qualities that she's looking for. For example, she might not be attracted to a man who is overweight, short, tall, or to a man with a specific skin color, whether white or black. Within our generally accepted norms, individuals still look for many specific traits. Now, what does this mean? There is nothing natural or existential about your individual preferences; they are simply that - your individual preferences. It's about your conditioning, how you have understood sexuality, and how you have been conditioned. Yes, some influences come from outside, like the influence of people - it may be fashionable to be with people who are thin, tall, fair-skinned, whatever it might be. But if you think about it, existence does not make any demarcation. That is why it accommodates all kinds of people, yet you have a preference.

If you can have such specific preferences, what is the problem in accepting that there are individuals whose preferences are even more specific? They are simply different from you. The moment we accept that there is nothing natural about our individual sexual preferences, we must acknowledge that sex is natural, our desire to connect with another human being is natural, and our desire to connect with our own sexuality is natural. Whatever expression it finds, the orientation aligns itself, its preferences are totally individualistic, and it is nobody's business to question the choice of an individual because that is his or her choice.

But again, where does this mindset come from? Why are we generally very edgy and fidgety about this subject? It's because somewhere the religious conditioning is still there in our minds. We have not gotten rid of it. It's not only the so-called religious people; even the so-called normal people, those who have identified their religious orientation and gone beyond it, still have not fully shaken off the conditioning of religion. Anything considered outside the bounds of what we have been led to believe as normal has been suppressed for thousands of years. Even now, for us, attraction is more physical than anything else.

When we hear about same-sex couples, the first thing that comes to mind is them having sex because we cannot visualize ourselves in that situation. There's immediate resentment because we cannot see it as normal behavior, compared to what we typically accept as normal. Again, why? Because religions have convinced us that the primary purpose of sex is reproduction. They do not discuss the full range of experiences that occur between sex and reproduction - there's romance, eroticism, role play, and a desire to shift identities. So much happens in sex that is not spoken about at all. For religion, sex is firstly condemned; because it's condemned, it must be spoken about as little as possible.

Now think about it - if there were no connection between sex and reproduction, these religious groups would have banned sex. They would have convinced governments that sex is a sin and would have banned it. People who displayed any interest in sex would have been punished. The only reason sex is tolerated is because it's the only process through which children can be produced, at least until now.

Naturally, our understanding of sex is very skewed and limited due to our social and religious conditioning. The moment we discard all this and simply view sex as an expression of individual freedom, as a desire to connect and to love, we see that the physical act is the last thing. There is an emotional connection. For example, when a woman feels attracted to another woman, it is not always physical. She might connect with another woman emotionally. These two women might naturally be drawn to each other, or they might be disillusioned with their relationships with men. What they were seeking in a relationship, they could not find with a man, who was perhaps too quick, too impulsive, too aggressive, and who did not understand the female body or her emotions. Now, what if she found all that she was looking for in a woman? That connection might eventually lead to what we recognize as sex, the merger of bodies to connect with something deeper, but there is so much that happens between the thought of being with another woman and actually being with her.

We can see this when we look at what we recognize as normal relationships - the physical aspect is only a small part. It's what we observe on the outside. We are thinking about it, having conversations in our minds, and envisioning ourselves as part of each other's lives. There's so much happening. Imagine, just because you are not part of that process, just because you're not thinking about all these things, going to a gay couple and saying, "What are you doing? This is wrong" sounds absurd to them because that is their world. They're not together just because they had an impulsive momentary awakening of "Oh, yes, I can be with this person." It's a process. It takes time, and the mind is deeply involved in it. The first misunderstanding comes from our external conditioning, mostly religious, and some of it social, and then from our own lack of understanding of the mind and the body. Human beings are sexual creatures. Sex is not an appendage; it's not an addition. It's the central force around which our lives revolve.

There is a passage in "Sex at Dawn" that, in a way, sums up human sexuality:

We have good news and bad news. The good news is that the dismal vision of human sexuality reflected in the standard narrative is mistaken. Men have not evolved to be deceitful cads, nor have millions of years shaped women into lying, two-timing gold diggers. But the bad news is that the amoral agencies of evolution have created in us a species with a secret it just can't keep. Homo sapiens evolved to be shamelessly, undeniably, inescapably sexual—lusty libertines, rakes, rogues, tomcats, and sex kittens; horndogs; bitches in heat.

We are sexual beings. The whole idea of a civilized, structured way of living - putting on a show, not revealing our true nature, suppressing our emotions - is all part of society. If you were to leave human beings to themselves, giving them their space and freedom, you would see that they express their sexuality in as many ways as you can possibly imagine. This is because sex is not limited to reproduction; it transcends physical bodies because it is deeper. More importantly, the pleasure we recognize is not external; it is internal. This is the single biggest misunderstanding about sex. If the pleasure you are seeking is inside you, then you can find any means, any avenue, to connect to it. That is where individuality comes from; that is where your orientation comes from. You are trying to find a channel through which you can connect with the pleasure, the bliss, that is already within you.

While it may seem like you're searching for pleasure in another person, it's actually not external. That's why you can pleasure yourself. That's why there is another orientation called self-orientation - where you're not even considering another partner. Perhaps you're not drawn to others, maybe you're fed up, maybe you don't have an opportunity, or perhaps you're married. It could be anything. You know that you can create pleasure for yourself. The possibility and the tools are within you. You have a body that can actually help you access it, and once you discover this, the world opens up. In fact, the journey outward happens later. Discovering that inner pleasure center happens first. Think about it: It is not through another body, not through watching or listening about sex, that you connect with your sexuality. You get in touch with it very early because it's your body. And you know some parts are different - they generate different sensations and, with some exploration, lead you all the way to that pleasure center. We often discover it accidentally because it is there. Then we start looking for it in other people. Our sexual orientation is shaped by our social structure, which also influences it.

If the social structure is restrictive, suppressing certain thoughts, you might not entertain those thoughts. Your orientation might revert to what we recognize as "normal." So, let us try to understand what happens in the mind that gives rise to our orientation. This is important to understand because you shouldn't feel like a victim of your sexual orientation. Even if you think something has gone wrong biologically, and your orientation has altered in ways you cannot explain, deep down, you should know it's your making - it's your life, your mind, your body. You can't blame it on nature, your parents, or biology. There is a part of you that you're unaware of - the subconscious, the unconscious, your mind, your dreams. Your orientation is being shaped there. Most of what you recognize as "you" is happening inside, not outside.

What does this mean? If you don't like the direction in which your orientation is moving - if you are a woman, naturally attracted to men, but also finding yourself attracted to women and you're beginning to notice it and, for whatever reason, you don't like it - it's still early stages. You shouldn't feel compelled to pursue a lifestyle you're unsure about. Know that you have a choice. You don't have to feel like you're suppressing your desires just because you choose not to entertain them.

We are living in a world where it is fashionable to declare that your orientation is unique. You need to recognize that often it just feels good to talk about it. But this is where understanding that your mind is involved in the process becomes crucial - you are shaping these orientations. It is not merely biological. You have a choice whether to pursue that direction and exercise that choice. There is nothing wrong with it. At the same time, there is absolutely nothing wrong with suppressing certain thoughts. We do it all the time. When our minds start moving in specific directions, we don't just let them run wild. We don't say, "Oh, this is natural." I mean, if you let the mind do everything it wants, it could drive you absolutely crazy.

This might sound harsh, but what is stopping the mind from imagining all kinds of orientations? What if you start feeling attracted to animals? I am one hundred percent certain that such a thought might have crossed our minds at some point, but it's so absurd that we don't entertain the thought. We exercise our choice and dismiss it as foolish, pulling ourselves back.

What happens if you're living in a social structure where such behavior is not only encouraged but glorified? Then, you might think, "Oh, it is natural. Maybe I am born to be attracted to cats." A day will come when people will start considering all these possibilities. In fact, it is already happening. There are individuals who feel they are genuinely attracted to certain animals. They might not think in terms of sex, but they believe they are cats or dogs. They alter their bodies. They start thinking they are another animal. If you were to question their choice, it would be the same as questioning the choice of gays or lesbians. Where do we draw the line? Can we even draw the line? Ultimately, it's about the individual and his choice. We cannot draw the line, but we can help people understand where this is coming from. It is not biological.

When you say you are trapped in another body - that you are a woman trapped in a man's body or a man trapped in a woman's body - that is delusional language. You are what you are. You're not trapped in another body. If you have a male body, you have a male body. It is just the body. You might have an orientation where you connect more with females, but that doesn't mean you are a female trapped in a male body. You have to use the right language. What this means is you are a male with a more female personality. If you are a woman but connect more with men, want to cut your hair short, dislike having breasts, want to walk like a man, smoke like a man, talk like a man - that doesn't mean you're not a woman. That doesn't mean you weren't born a woman. How can you live with the idea that you are trapped in a woman's body?

The way to avoid all this confusion is to watch the mind and to bring more awareness to your desires and inclinations. Like any other preference, if you leave everything to your mind, it will consume itself. For example, the mind loves food - and there might have been times when your mind entertained the thought of eating human meat. You've heard that human meat is actually very sweet. But why don't you exercise that choice? Meat is meat, right? Why not human meat? Because it is wrong, socially unacceptable, and simply foolish. All these reasons converge to tell us not to entertain those thoughts. Even before you start entertaining that thought seriously, you dismiss it. But at least once, the thought might have crossed your mind. I'm sure many of us have thought about it, but we don't go biting the hand of our partners to check. We know some things are just plain stupid.

This extends to our sexuality as well. Not every form of sexuality has to be entertained just because it is different, feels good, or is cool and fashionable. It is still your choice, your mind, and your body. You can decide. If you are suppressing certain sexual desires because of society, that is wrong. Similarly, expressing certain sexual desires simply because society wants you to is also wrong. Both actions belong to the same domain, and you need to be aware of this. Suppression is wrong because it's unnatural. At the same time, expression can also be wrong because it might be detrimental to your way of life, especially if that expression is just a momentary, impulsive outburst. Not all sexual orientations develop gradually; not all are sustained by the mind and body; not all have strong supporting structures. Some arise merely for social satisfaction. Yes, a bit of orientation is there, but you are exercising a choice.

Thus, understanding the dynamics of same-sex relationships involves bringing our awareness to the mind, the body, and the influences of the world. Ultimately, the choice should be left to the individual. No social group, religious group, or political organization should have any say in this matter because it is complex. What's happening inside an individual is intricate and deeply connected with their personal identities. Interfering from the outside means you are tampering with their core processes of life. At most, you can illuminate and educate people about what's happening on the inside. You can teach kids about the nature of the mind, why the mind is not always helpful, why you need to be cautious of what the mind is telling you, and why you shouldn't act on every single impulse that crosses your mind. This is a natural process of developing awareness in children.

That is all we can do as a society. But once they become adults, you don't have a choice but to accept their orientation. This applies to families, communities, and everyone involved. If your child comes out and says, "This is who I am," regardless of the language they use, if that is their preference, you have no other choice but to accept it. You will cause more damage by rejecting their orientation, condemning it, or pushing them away. And that is where you need to make a choice. What is more important to you - your church or your child? If you can't even distinguish between what is more important, then you need to question your right to call yourself a parent. Your first responsibility is to your child, not to your church. And if your child is telling you something and you're unable to listen, then what is the point? It is a complex subject; many factors are involved, but there is no need to complicate it further.

Life is Fluid

A few basic rules need to be understood. There are many things in life, in nature, in existence, that we cannot fit into the boxes of our understanding. Life is fluid. Existence is fluid. Human choices are fluid. With the openness and human intelligence we are endowed with, we possess tremendous tools that animals don't have. We can sit and have a conversation. How many differences can we clear up just by talking? This is where the problem lies. If talking about something, if discussing something openly is suppressed, that's where the problem starts. From there, everything else falls apart. If you are unable to openly talk about your sexual orientation, if you are unable to openly express your desires, that's where the problem is. You are not given an opportunity to understand, to compare your choices with multiple viewpoints, or to listen to multiple arguments. That is why we have a phrase called "coming out of the closet." Think about it. It isn't natural to sit in a closet, with no dialogue, no discussion. Whatever your mind is telling you becomes your reality.

Imagine you've kept your identity questions to yourself for fifteen years before finally declaring, "Well, I've been thinking about this, and now I believe this is who I am." What if you came out of the closet as soon as the thought arose, and started talking about it? You could have been introduced to different ways of looking at it. Discussing them openly could have exposed you to various perspectives on your identity. Unfortunately, few resources, such as books or specific library sections, are available to explore such orientations in a scientific, biological, philosophical, or spiritual context. This lack of information often forces you back to social media groups, where deeper discussions are scarce. These platforms might allow you to share what you're feeling, but they often function as closed groups without much meaningful exchange.

Unless we bring these discourses out into the open, unless they become natural, casual conversations just the way you talk about your hair, your skin, your children, anything related to your physical body - if you are able to talk about your sexual orientation, then there's more awareness. With more awareness, you have more choices. Then you don't need someone else telling you what to do and what not to do, because you can make the choices for yourself.

In ancient Hindu scriptures, there is mention of different orientations. For example, although it does not explicitly mention any orientations apart from what we recognize as normal, all the methods of pleasuring oneself and their partners can be applied to any sex. This is because the majority of it has nothing to do with the actual act of sex, what we recognize as penetration. Most of what we recognize as sex happens before penetration - the foreplay, the involvement of emotions, the involvement of bodies - which has nothing to do with the actual orientation. You can find an expression for almost all the different activities identified as ways of enhancing your sex life; they can be applied to anybody. Two women can apply it to each other, two men can apply it to each other, and you can apply it to anybody, anything. Why? Because it is a natural expression to connect with eroticism.

MEDITATION AND SEX

Eroticism has nothing to do with sex per se. It is a pleasure center; in fact, it is not even just restricted to the body. It is the ultimate pleasure center. It is also the quest of spirituality and meditation. I would go as far as to say that even choosing to become a meditator, to take a meditative path to bliss, is in a way choosing a kind of sexual orientation because the ultimate bliss you experience in meditation is similar to an orgasm. However, in meditation, you are experiencing it with a lot more freedom, less dependency on the physical body, and you are able to get to that place of limitless bliss, visit it whenever you want, and experience it as much as you want. Meditation is my sexual orientation. I have chosen to find it within me directly because I became aware of such a process.

The problem with most people is that they're not introduced to meditation in this way. Imagine if meditation were taught as both the most fashionable and the oldest form of sexual orientation. Think about it: If you were to tell Buddhists that Buddha's meditation was his sexual preference, they might be shocked or even outraged. This is because in our minds, the words "sex" and "meditation" represent two completely different concepts. However, existentially, they are one and the same. How can there be two different forms of pleasure? There are different ways of connecting to it, but the pleasure itself is the same. Whether you're eating an apple or a mango - two different fruits with different tastes - both touch the same center of pleasure. They're not two different things.

The moment we understand that pleasure is a center - not created, not manufactured, but already there - we realize that we can access it in as many different ways as possible. We can reach it by having sex, regardless of our preference; we can connect with it through food, alcohol, drugs, sports, creativity, or meditation.

Ultimately, if we understand that we are all trying to connect with something, we realize that we're not attempting to manufacture or create things. There is something within us that is longing to be found and discovered, and we're all trying to find it in different ways. We use different words and ways of expressing it, but when you look at humanity in totality, you will see that differences are only at the level of language. At the fundamental level, sexual energy is universal, and connecting with it is a fundamental desire. This desire transcends the mind and the body; it is existential. Our orientations and preferences are unique; this is where we become individuals. That is why an individual's choice to connect to that bliss by sitting quietly, doing nothing, not engaging in sexual activity, must be respected just as much as a man who seeks it with a woman, or a woman who seeks it with another woman. Every method must be respected because it is their individual choice to connect in their own way.

There's no need to hide our sexual orientation. Conversations and acceptance should start as soon as you begin to discover these things. For your own sake, for your happiness, and for your contentment, it is necessary to talk about what's happening on the inside. Then, despite sharing it and getting multiple viewpoints, if you are clear and certain that this is your orientation, that is your choice - exercise it openly, without any fear. However, if you are unsure, do not exercise the choice just because it's fashionable; you may regret it because it was not truly your choice, but rather imposed from the outside without you realizing it.

The moment you drop the fear of what's running through your mind - which could be perceived as crazy - you should start having conversations. Talk with your family members, talk with your friends. They might think you're crazy, but it's better to let that "craziness" come out so that it can be seen by others, and then you can evaluate how crazy or how natural it really is. Without these conversations, if you keep everything inside and suddenly come out of the closet, you haven't allowed for multiple perspectives to evaluate your choices. For all you know, you might be wrong. And even if you're right, such a sudden announcement can be shocking to your family and community, who have built a life on a certain understanding.

All this confusion clears up if conversations are already a part of your narrative. Then nothing is sudden. You don't have to sneak out of the closet; you can accept it openly whenever you're ready because it's already out there. By doing this, you not only help yourself, but those around you in accepting what is generally regarded as unusual or not normal. As long as it's your choice, coming from you, and you have evaluated it through conversations, intelligence, and awareness, then it is nobody's business to question that choice.

Orgasm

Divine Harmony

How can I reconcile my sexual desires with my religious beliefs? Is there any connection between sex and religion?

There is a very close connection between sex and religion, sort of like the relationship between a cat and a mouse. Sex has always been condemned by religions, with religion often displaying a fear of sex. The relationship between them is viciously life-negating. The moment you recognize a religion as organized, you'll see that it has condemned sex, without exception. Christianity has been at the forefront in terms of the sheer intensity with which it has opposed sex and the openness with which it has criticized it. Its unapologetic nature in how it regards sex makes it unique in human history.

The "Original Sin"

The doctrine of the world's largest religion states that Jesus, their savior, was born of a virgin birth. What does that mean? Never before has such a concept been recorded anywhere in human history - a birth so unique. How can there be a virgin birth by the very definition of the word "virgin"? If your mother is a virgin, then you should not exist. You are here because she is not a virgin; you are here because she had sex. It's the most basic understanding from a fifth-grade science class: birth takes place after sex, after intercourse, after conception.

Yet here is a doctrine that is the founding platform on which all other belief systems and understandings of life, mind, body, your place in the scheme of things, and what happens after death are based. The founding principle of the world's largest religion rests on the claim that Jesus had a virgin birth. Mary was not only a virgin; even her hymen was not ruptured. That is how pure she is. And this is how grossly they interpret life. Why such animosity against sex? What is the problem? What would have happened if they had accepted the simple fact that whether he's called a savior or not, whether he's recognized as the son of God or something else, what is the problem in acknowledging that he was born like everybody else?

The problem is that the entire foundation of the religion is built on the basic premise that sex is a sin. The understanding of sex as sin comes first - Jesus comes later. They had to call him the son of God and say that he took a virgin birth because a normal birth is recognized as a sin. Merely being born is seen as committing a crime. Adam and Eve were banished from the Garden of Eden for having sex. What was their crime? Simply recognizing the most basic of life forces and acknowledging the most basic of human instincts got them kicked out of the Garden of Eden. From then on, they lived in shame. The Garden of Eden represents nothing but the realm of life we occupy, what we recognize as reality. The forbidden fruit is nothing but sex. And what is the punishment? You are told that you are a sinner, already condemned. The rest of your time here on earth, you must do things to atone for that sin. It's a clever and cunning way of saying that you don't have any moral authority to shape your life the way you want to. You are a prisoner, a convicted felon in the eyes of the church, in the eyes of God. Your freedom is dictated by them. You can move around, you can do certain things, but you have to come every week and give your attendance, just so that they know you have not left the city without their permission.

It's essentially saying you are out on parole. You're not free. How can you be free? You were born, and it wasn't a virgin birth. There was only one man deemed free because he supposedly had a virgin birth, a clean birth; your birth is impure. Your very birth is seen as a crime. If this is not manipulation, if this is not trickery or deceit designed to control the mind and actions of Man, then what is it? Christianity is just one example. We see this theme in almost every other religion. No religion openly accepts sex as a natural part of life. While some religions may not openly condemn sex, they don't address it at all.

Take Buddhism, for example. They don't talk about sex. They don't explain what it is. They don't shed light on what it involves. Now, how can you expect to awaken a group of people and offer them a path that leads them beyond the strife and struggles of life if you are not helping them understand what is actually keeping them in bondage? If the purpose of religion is to liberate, then it must directly address the shackles. What is stopping you from realizing your true nature? What is keeping you in bondage? Where are you spending most of your time and energy? Where are your life resources draining?

It is not hard to see that human society is obsessed with sex. This is where all the energies are invested - in marriage, in children, in ensuring that you get the best possible sex you can. There's no beating around the bush. Human society is organized around one and only one principle: The richer you are, the more successful you are, the better the sex. That's it. Take away sex, and the whole thing collapses. There is nothing left to strive for. Just imagine if you were to announce that there is no such thing as marriage from now on. Hypothetically, let's assume that each individual is totally free - free to be with anybody they want for as long as they want, with everything mutually agreed upon. There are no laws that bind you. You are free, and sex is divine. The more sex you have, the more you are connecting with your divine nature. Let's assume hypothetically that this is the narrative that is spread.

Let's imagine a new religion comes along that is obsessed with sex. It loves sex, teaches about it, talks about it, and has removed all the guilt associated with it. All the guilt one feels when they look at themselves in the mirror because their body is sexual is gone. The dichotomy is removed, all that conflict is gone, and then you wake up in this new world where sex is neither a mysterious taboo subject that you must discuss in private, nor is it unnecessarily glorified because everybody is talking about it. It's out in the open. There is nothing drawing you towards it unnaturally; when there is a desire, it is readily available. Well, sex should be the most easily available thing on the planet because human beings are the most easily available beings. If sex were something that grew on a special tree, only in a special season, then yes, there would have to be competition, struggle, and a hierarchy determining who gets to experience that rarity. But it's in all of us; it's everywhere. There would be no necessity to organize your life around sex.

If this were to happen, then what is the meaning of success? What is the meaning of achievement? What is the meaning of all the false names and designations we chase after? This doesn't mean that we will become useless. It doesn't mean that we won't create. It doesn't mean that we'll simply waste our lives idling. It's exactly the opposite. Individuals will become more energized, more invigorated because all that energy that was wasted on thinking about sex, trying to obtain it, and secretly engaging in it, is now available for your creativity, your spiritual growth, and your enlightenment. With a single snap of a finger, the whole of humanity could be transformed. Just by accepting that we are sex - there can be no separation between a human being and the process through which they come into this world.

How can you liberate humanity when you are condemning the very channel, the very process through which you take birth? There is no meaning to the word "human" without two individuals coming together, without the exchange of those energies, without sex. Now, how can you condemn sex and claim to help an individual reach paradise? Isn't that the greatest lie that religions have been telling Man - don't talk about that one thing, that one thing that can actually help you understand life, that one thing that can actually liberate you? Don't talk about that; let's talk about this other liberation. What other liberation? There is no other freedom. A mind that is filled with sex is a mind that is imprisoned; it is operating based on the desires of an entity other than yourself. You have given control of your life to something else. If that is not addressed, if you are not freed from that bondage, then all other attempts to liberate you must be a lie. It is not that religions hate sex; they only pretend to. It is important to understand this.

If you look at the individual lives of these so-called religious men and women, their minds are filled with sex. Occasionally, we see this exploding, coming out in all its glorious colors, showing how perverted a simple idea of sex has become in a mind that has tried to deny it. Sex is not a simple, isolated phenomenon of life that you can put in a separate room, lock it, and forget about. It is a fundamental driving force of life. Your body craves sex because it is sexual; it has come from sex, and in a way, its purpose is sex. That is why the desire exists. You cannot simply tell the body, "Now I have become religious, stop thinking about sex. It's not that important. It's a sin." The more you condemn it, the more it will find an outlet elsewhere.

If you deny the body its right to express its sexuality, it will find its expression in the mind. What is the mind at the end of the day? The deepest layers of our mind are occupied by our strongest desires, desires that torment us, that push and pull us. Our subconscious is filled with our deepest fears, our deepest desires, and our greatest longings. It is the body, when it has the ability to express itself, when it has the freedom to be itself without any condemnation or guilt, that frees the mind. There is an outlet. The body is the outlet for the mind to release some of the things that are not needed.

Sex cannot be merely a mental concept. If it starts becoming just that, then everything you see will be colored by it. You will never be able to see a human being for who they truly are. You will never be able to see life for what it is. It becomes a smokescreen that blocks everything because your mind is clouded. In a way, it is always searching for sex and not getting it. Consequently, your entire life becomes disconnected, filled with a dissatisfied longing for something that is your birthright. What happens when you are denied the very thing for which you are here? Everything else starts to fall apart; then life becomes just about covering up.

The birth of hypocrisy in humanity is the contamination of sex. How can a man or woman be honest with themselves, about their bodies, their desires, and their intentions when that honesty is punished? When that honesty is recognized as perversion? If you were to openly express your desire for sex and the intensity and frequency with which you desire it, you would be labeled a pervert, as if there's something wrong with you. Why are you thinking about sex so much? It is because the desire is existential. It is there. It appears overwhelming not because it is inherently so, but because we have condemned sex and pushed it into the mental sphere, making it a constant preoccupation. This is the biggest contribution of religions: First, they induce guilt, then they offer you a solution. You must first be made to feel like a sinner, and only then can you seek forgiveness. Only then can you go begging, crawling on the floor. Otherwise, you would walk with confidence and certainty.

Condemning sex is like breaking the back of an individual. You first break his back and then offer him solutions, questioning why he is unable to walk. You then create theology after theology explaining why he's unable to walk. If religion is offering a solution, it is addressing a problem that it created in the first place. Without it, there would be no problem. Without the condemnation of sex, there would be no sinners, no need for salvation, no need for atonement. People would be free. How can you turn to an institution professing to have the answers for your life when you are already filled with freedom? It is only when you are in shackles that you seek help.

Otherwise, there is no necessity at all. It is the same mentality that condemns sex that also condemns all other expressions of sex.

Sex Isn't Just for Reproduction

The moment you deny such a basic scientific principle of life, you have to be against science. Then all your other explanations of these vital processes of life will also be twisted; your understanding will be aligned with your beliefs. There is no basis whatsoever for speaking against abortion or birth control. The argument given is that a life is being destroyed. Consider the absurdity of this argument: you are concerned about a life that has not yet happened, about a life that is about to happen, and in that process, you're destroying the freedom and autonomy of a life that is already here. If an individual does not have the choice to give birth or not, to be pregnant or not, to have sex without it leading to pregnancy, if they cannot make arrangements to enjoy the act of sex without worrying about childbirth, then you're denying that basic right. Right there, you're condemning the very process; it's, in fact, an extension of the condemnation of sex. Because you condemn sex, you also have to condemn birth control. Allowing birth control would mean you're saying you can have sex as much as you want, without the fear of giving birth that might stop someone from having sex.

Imagine if there were no contraceptives - there was no such thing as birth control. People would be terrified of sex. How many children can you realistically care for? The reason you can enjoy sex without worrying about children is that we are intelligent enough to use birth control. It's not at all surprising that the world's largest religion, except for small pockets of so-called liberal Christian churches, is fundamentally against abortion. In 1984, in Washington, a man named Curtis Beseda firebombed a women's health clinic and abortion center. When asked why, he said he did it "in the glory of God." That same year, twenty-four other abortion clinics were bombed. Almost one hundred and fifty cases were reported. Just the idea that abortion is against someone's religious beliefs has fueled this violence. Those who are engaged in providing abortions are labeled as sinners, as evil.

There cannot be a legitimate argument against sex. If you present an argument against sex, no matter how cleverly that argument is organized and arranged, it eventually will be regarded as a crime against humanity. Condemning sex should be seen as the biggest crime, even greater than murder, in my opinion. Because in murder, you're ending one life; in condemning sex, you are destroying the possibility of life for generations to come. You are obliterating the possibility of natural living. You are creating an environment filled with guilt, suspicion, and mistrust. Where do we get these words from - "cheating?" Think about it. If a human being decides to have sex with someone outside of marriage, it is regarded as cheating. That means you are acknowledging that marriage is just a game, because in this game, cheating is not allowed. You are already accepting that marriage is not existential; it is a game that we are playing, and it is the rules that we have agreed to follow. It has nothing to do with life. Now, if that game is against the fundamental processes of life, if those rules oppose the flow of natural life, then how can you adhere to those rules without killing something inside of you? That is why just because two individuals are married doesn't mean they are not thinking about sex.

In America, after toasters, the single biggest electrical appliance sold is vibrators. Let that sink in. And mind you, a vibrator is not a toy. It is a necessity for many people because we have created such an unnatural environment for sex, condemning it so much that people have to find other ways of connecting with it. Just imagine a human being - a full-blooded, conscious, wonderful being capable of all kinds of expressions - using an electrical appliance to stimulate some of the most sensitive, most delicate parts of their body. If that is not an injustice, then what is? If someone cannot look at that and say we need to free human beings, then we have seriously mistaken what sex is. We have misunderstood it. We have blindly accepted a totally wrong idea of sex, that it is only an avenue for childbirth. No. Sex is something more. It is existential.

Unless individuals are given total freedom - and of course, freedom in sex doesn't mean you can just go and have sex with anybody and everybody - it is about mutual agreement. That is what freedom means: respecting your freedom as well as the freedom of your partner. This whole idea that free sex destroys society is one of the dumbest ideas out there. There is no basis in science or reality for an idea like that. Free sex doesn't mean that we become like animals. We still have our minds, our intelligence, and our choices. We don't have to unnaturally attach ourselves to someone after the desire for sex wanes. It doesn't mean that the desire will wane in every case, but when it does, if you are unable to acknowledge that and move on, then what is that relationship if not an abusive one? People are stuck in abusive relationships because they are taught that breaking a marriage is a sin, while simultaneously being taught that thinking about having sex with multiple people is wrong. If this is not hypocrisy, then what is the meaning of the word "hypocrisy?" And this is what defines human society - the way we have organized our lives, the way we treat each other.

Whether you are born a woman, a man, or whatever you are born as, it doesn't matter - you recognize your sexuality. It is impossible for an individual to say, "I don't have any sexuality." We don't have individuals who claim, "I don't have any orientation. I don't have any interest in sex." Some orientations are easily understandable, while some take a little more courage to accept, but the orientation and the desire are there. Now think about it. The recognition that two individuals of the same sex can actually enjoy sex - isn't that proof that sex has nothing to do with childbirth? Sex is so much more than just for childbirth. Otherwise, how can we explain the sexual orientations of gays and lesbians?

Again, it is not at all surprising that religions are reluctant to acknowledge the existence of such orientations. Individuals are screaming at the top of their voices, "It is me. It is my body. I have recognized it. I see it." Yes, there might be cases where it is simply mental, but you cannot deny that individuals can have their unique orientations. A man need not always be attracted to a woman. A woman need not always be attracted to a man because attraction has nothing to do with childbirth. Sex has nothing to do with childbirth. It is an existential energy finding its expression through form. When we talk about attractiveness, there are many theories explaining why certain traits are recognized as attractive and why certain traits are not.

Law of Attraction

What attracts a woman to a man? You might hear complex theories like she's looking for a healthy male to produce children, or she's seeking safety and security. But at the most basic level, what is the attraction? The attraction is always to form and symmetry, which is how we recognize beauty. The way we recognize beauty in life and nature is exactly the same way we recognize beauty in our partners. The more proportional and symmetrical the body, the more appealing it is - it's actually that simple. It's not that complicated.

Our human mind is conditioned to recognize beauty in symmetry. It's just like when you look at a flower; if a few petals are missing, there is a disconnect. You would naturally gravitate towards those flowers which are intact. Now, this has nothing to do with sex. Attraction towards another body need not always be sexual. Being drawn towards beautiful forms need not always involve sexual desire. We are drawn to beautiful things because it resonates with the mind. It has nothing to do with the body; sexuality, however, is a bodily phenomenon. The mind cooperates with it, presenting it with images and experiences, but the mind itself can have orientations, likes, and dislikes, independent of the body's sexuality.

If you don't understand this, you will never fully grasp orientations beyond the traditionally accepted ones. You assume a man is attracted to a woman and a woman to a man because you have intermixed both the desires of the mind and the body, viewing them as one entity. In the modern world, there is a greater propensity for disconnection between the mind and the body. That is why we are seeing newer ways of orienting now in modern society.

It is not at all a surprise that the mind is able to find its own expression independent of the body. And nobody can call that perversion. How can your mind be a perversion? It's your own mind. When you condemn sex, you end up having to condemn everything. Naturally, your understanding of sex is so dead, so one-dimensional, that it can't accommodate all its nuances.

What is the relationship between religion and sex? It's a hostile relationship. Can you reconcile your religious beliefs with your sexual desires? As long as your religion condemns sex, you cannot reconcile it. Trying to find common ground between a religious belief that condemns sex and a mind and body that love sex is not going to happen. You will spend your whole life frustrated. You will either satisfy your religion or satisfy yourself. There cannot be a middle ground. Those who think they have found a nice middle ground are only fooling themselves. Their own lives, their level of pain, and their level of frustration are testimonies to the failed reconciliation of a religious belief that is opposed to sex.

This misunderstanding of sex is also at the heart of the problem of men not understanding women. Many men do not grasp a simple fact: women's sexuality is different. The time it takes for her to enter into a sexual state of mind, for her body to be aroused, for her mind to be aroused, follows different trajectories from that of a man. Even this basic understanding is lacking in the majority of men. They don't consider the other side of sex - the most important side - their partner's desires, their partner's pleasure. Why? Because of the condemnation of sex. It's all connected. Once you label something as sin, then understanding it becomes a sin, and even having a conversation with your partner becomes fraught. Asking her, "What is it that you want me to do?" How often does a man ask this question to a woman? He has no right to even touch her without asking this question. "What should I do? What do you like? What do you not like?" He assumes everything. He assumes that just because he is a man, she must be interested in him. And that is why he's a jerk. That is why women don't like jerks. They need something more. A basic question: "What do you like? What do you not like?"

The conversation is now entering into the sexual sphere. For thousands of years, women have endured this crippled understanding of sex. Just imagine the pain, the frustration, the torture a woman has to endure when a man does not understand the ABCs of sex, when he is only interested in what *he* wants. Ian Kerner shares in his book "She Comes First":

Studies show that three-fourths of men are finished with sex within a few minutes of starting. But women often need fifteen minutes or more to become sufficiently aroused for orgasm. And therein lies a world of rage, grief, and airborne pots and pans.

To put it in grammatical terms, Most women are left frustrated with "incomplete sentences" in the face of their partners' prematurely dangling participles.

Something has gone wrong, but it wasn't always like this. There was a time when a woman and her sexuality were at the center of understanding sex. A man's desire for sex revolved around the woman. She was the undisputed queen of sex because her sexuality was more vibrant, deeper, and it encompassed all the multidimensional aspects of life. It touched the emotional, the physical, and the mental spheres. Her intuitive understanding of sex was deeper. Men respected and valued that. There was a time when it was the woman who called all the shots during sex. Remnants of this culture still exist; we can find them in the scriptures. Why isn't this mainstream? Because the mainstream understanding of sex comes from the so-called mainstream religions that have already perverted the understanding of sex in favor of men. So, all those examples, all those stories where women's sexuality held a central position are simply left out.

There is an interesting tale in the "Cradle of Erotica." It is written that during the Tang dynasty, Empress Wu Zetian ruled China. She understood that sex and power were inexorably linked, and she decreed that government officials and visiting dignitaries must pay homage to her imperial highness by performing cunnilingus upon her. No joke. Old paintings depict the beautiful, powerful empress standing and holding her ornate robe open while a high nobleman or diplomat is shown kneeling before her, applying his lips and tongue to her royal mound.

Is there a connection between sex and religion? Yes, there is a connection. If you strip away all the distortions, all the subtle and gross manipulations to make sex masculine, and approach sex as the pure existential expression it is, you will find a connection. You will see that sex is the highest form of religiousness. If religiousness is about searching for something beyond, if it is about understanding your mind and body, if it is a way to cleanse your past, to forget your future, so that you can be in the present moment, then there is no other activity, no other human expression, that can be regarded as superior to sex. Sex is the highest, because in sex lies the complete path, the complete method to transform your limited, restricted human existence into an expression of consciousness and aliveness. Sex alone can transform you completely.

The further back you go in time, the more you will see the whole idea of marriage, the whole idea of two individuals coming together and staying in a committed relationship longer than necessary, longer than simply their pleasures dictated, happened because they were helping each other grow spiritually. Sex wasn't just for pleasure. It wasn't just for entertainment. When you understand that it is a pathway to grow spiritually, then it is natural that you would opt for a longer committed relationship because there's so much understanding being exchanged, and understanding being built. It makes sense to stay committed. That is the only realm - only when marriage is recognized as spiritual, only when two individuals come together with a full understanding that they are attracted to each other, that they will use this attractiveness to help each other grow spiritually. Only in such an understanding does long-term commitment make sense.

That is where we deviate from animals. The moment we forget spiritual growth and simply hold on to the outer covering that we recognize as marriage - the husk, ignoring the actual kernel, the actual purpose for which two individuals have come together, we end up with frustrated marriages and discontented relationships. Why? Because they're not helping each other grow. They have forgotten that they came together to grow. There is a deep connection between sex and religiousness. Sex is the journey that you undertake to reach the destination of religiousness, to get to that mysterious space, to that transcendental realm within you. You only need some help - the mind of your partner, the body of your partner, the love that you share, and the attraction that you have for each other. The sheer intensity of the connection you share helps you to transcend your own limited ego, your own limited mind. In that sense, a relationship is a cleansing process. If you're too filled with yourself, too stuck in your ego, you cannot accommodate the other. Now, how can you grow spiritually if you are unable to accommodate the other? Spiritual growth should be the central idea around which relationships revolve. With that understanding, we can accommodate all kinds of sexualities because conversation and mutual understanding become more important than just our fixed ideas of what sex is. Religion has to be kept as far away from sex as possible. Religion is totally blind to the spectacular force that is sex. It does not see it, it does not understand it. There's no need to try and reconcile your religious beliefs with your sexual desires. They are totally different and must remain separate.

From Sacred to Scandalous

Why is sex so misunderstood and perverted? What went wrong?

In human society, sex is a victim of civilization. We need to understand some tectonic shifts in how human beings have evolved compared to how other animals live in nature. Something is very different about human beings. The difference is unmistakable. In certain areas, this difference is enlightening and profound - our ability to use language, create music, and contemplate something higher. These are activities we proudly associate with the word "human." Yet, there is another dimension where we are lower than even animals: we are disconnected from life in a literal sense, living as if the basic laws of life don't apply to us. We engage in behaviors that defy common sense.

Human sexuality is where both these dimensions find their expression. On the one hand, our sexuality is nothing like that of animals; it involves more sophistication, more connection, more emotional involvement, and a deeper understanding of sex.

Despite this, our basic grasp of what sex is - and what it isn't - is totally lacking.

We search for things in sex that we can never find in sex. We put so much burden on a simple act - a phenomenon that is meant to be liberating, something that is meant to remind you that you are here to play. There's no other activity that reminds us that we are children quite like sex. It is one of the least sophisticated of activities. You don't have to be well-versed in the language of sex, be an expert in the art of sex, or have a college degree to know how to have sex. You don't need instructions or guidance; you only need innocence and child-like curiosity. It is a total misunderstanding to think that lack of sex education results in perversions. Not at all. Sex is like breathing - who taught you how to breathe? Which school did you go to learn how to breathe? It is such a natural process; your body knows what it's doing, and your mind is aware of what's happening. The less educated you are in matters of sex, the less perverted your understanding of sex, the more natural it is.

The "Devolution" of Sex

The easiest way to understand this is to look at our own evolution from hunter-gatherers to farmers, to men and women of the industrial revolution, and then as creatures of the technological revolution. Sex remains the same. The desire for sex has always been the same. The bliss that an individual experiences hasn't changed. But because Man has been changing, his environment has been changing, his social structure has been changing - all that has had a tremendous influence on his sex life. It has greatly influenced the way he approaches sex, what he desires from it, and how he sees himself as a creature bound by the laws of sex. The simpler your understanding of life, the simpler the social structure, the simpler your understanding of sex.

Over time, Man's idea of sex has not become simpler; it has become more complicated. It has acquired its own alternate reality, so much so that it must be restricted to a certain private space. The basic differentiation between man and woman is recognized in the word "sex." If you take away sex, there is no difference between a man and a woman. As creatures of existence, we are one and the same. And yet, how starkly do we see this difference? How obvious is the difference between a man and a woman? It is the first thing we notice. It is the most immediate thing our attention is drawn to. This very differentiation comes from sex, from our desire for it. And yet, for us, the word "sex" is taboo. As a human society, we have condemned the word. We have perverted that word itself. You cannot openly talk about sex. If someone hears you using the word "sex," you will get immediate attention. It does not matter what you're saying; you could be saying "I don't like sex," and still that'll get attention. Why? Because we have tried to hide it as best as we can. Great effort has been undertaken, a concerted effort to ensure that sex remains as invisible as possible. Human civilization, in one dimension, can be understood by its desire to hide sex.

The institutions it believes in, the ideas it holds on to, the values it teaches can all be traced back to this one overarching desire: to hide sex. It starts from the story of Adam and Eve. That whole story is about hiding sex. Adam and Eve were playing in the Garden of Eden. Firstly, I wonder why they called it a garden, because if it is a natural, pristine environment, why would you call it a garden? A garden is a cultivated place. Maybe the Garden of Eden was such a place where sex was forbidden. No, Adam and Eve became aware of themselves. The word used is they "knew" each other. The word "knew" literally meant they had sex with each other. "Knowing" wasn't just about saying hello and introducing yourselves; in the biblical sense, "knowing" literally meant knowing each other inside out, knowing each other's bodies, and knowing each other's minds, which happens only through sex. They knew each other, and they became aware of their sexuality. They became aware of their bodies.

The body is only used as a metaphor for sex. It is not their bodies they were ashamed of; they were ashamed of their sex, their act, and that is why they hid their genitals using fig leaves.

You can see that this whole story comes from a dimension very far removed from reality, very far from the natural processes of life - what is natural to the mind, what is natural to the body, what is natural to a human being. This is a story that tries to turn something natural into something unnatural. Why is there a necessity to be punished for eating from the tree of knowledge? And what is the tree of knowledge if not sex?

It is through sex that you are given a glimpse of the beyond, where you can realize there is something more to you than just your body. In all other activities, your body and mind are present, involved, always there. Thus, there is no way for you to experience anything transcendental, directly. You cannot gain a direct spiritual experience through any other means. You can hear about it, you can talk about it, but just like if you have never tasted an apple, you will never truly know what it tastes like. You could read a hundred books on what an apple tastes like, but at the end of it, your actual understanding of what an apple is would not have improved at all.

It is through sex that you get the actual taste of the beyond because it is an unforgettable experience. It is a moment when you are not there - your mind is gone, your body is gone. For that brief moment, everything disappears: your body, your partner's body, the place where you are, the world around you, people's judgments, your stress, your worries - all are gone in a single moment. Now, that is what we experience as bliss. We don't know what else to call it. It is simply an experience where everything you've been experiencing is taken away in a single moment. It is the end of experience.

Experience No Experience

Orgasm is an experience of no experience. You are experiencing a non-experience for the first time. It is so blissful because your life is filled with moments of pain, moments of strain, and your body is constantly in a state of disturbance. Your body is in pain at every level, subtle and gross. And what do you do through the act of sex? You fully engage your body in the act of sex. Every part of you participates - every sense is activated, your entire body and mind are involved. Lots of energy is expended as you immerse yourself deeply in the experience, and what you experience as orgasm is that single moment when all the stress and strain your body has been experiencing - whether for the last twenty minutes, thirty minutes, or an hour - is suddenly gone.

Sex is the perfect mechanism to introduce you to a higher spiritual concept: that suffering is inevitable in life, even in the greatest acts of pleasure. You cannot experience pleasure without experiencing pain. This is the nature of reality, the duality of life; pain and pleasure go hand in hand. That is the first realization you come to. There's more pain in getting sex than you actually think about - emotional pain, psychological pain. It is not merely a simple act of connecting with someone; something deeper is happening there. In a single moment, all that pain, all that physical exertion becomes pleasure. So, you learn that pain and pleasure are intertwined, and they belong to the body. And then, in that same instant, you are also introduced to a part of you that has nothing to do with the mind or the body - where you exist but not as a mind or a body.

This is why, even if you approach sex casually, even if you see it as just a simple release of stress and tension, or even if you engage in it playfully, what you experience at the end of it is always profound. Irrespective of how you approach sex, you're not denied the bliss because it is not your choosing; it is not your body's choosing; it is not your mind's choosing. It is existential. Sex is a ritual, a sacred ritual, a divine communion between two bodies that are in different states of energy levels - one in a giving mode and the other in a receiving mode. There is a beautiful dance of giving and receiving. There are moments when the male is giving, and there are moments when the female is giving, and the roles are reversed. It's a pure exchange of energies.

For a moment, if you stop visualizing sex as just physical, if you stop seeing the bodies and enter the inner dimension of sex, you will see what a churning it is, what a transformative process it is. The sheer exhilaration of sex, the sheer intensity of it, requires a totally different explanation than simply saying it's for producing babies. That is our biological understanding of sex. Why do we have sex? Why do animals have sex? So they can multiply, so they can produce offspring.

With this basic assumption, we explain human sexuality, promiscuity, and monogamy, and why human beings prefer the types of sex and the types of partners they do. Everything is explained in terms of the necessity to reproduce. For example, when a woman is attracted to a man, she is supposedly looking at the health of the man, his physical strength, thinking about her offspring, evaluating if this man is capable of producing the right kind of babies for her. Now, this is our biological understanding. Anyone who knows anything about sex understands that they're not thinking about all these things during the act. It's not even there as a subtext in the mind. Reproduction is a tiny part of sex. It is an inconsequential part.

Whether you are reproducing or not, your desire for sex is always there. That is why your desire for sex doesn't just evaporate after you produce babies. Your desire for sex doesn't reduce after you enter a committed monogamous relationship, although there's enough evidence to suggest that interest levels in sex can diminish. Married couples are most interested in sex during the early stages of their marriage. This is an observed, documented fact. They don't have more and more sex as time passes; it only diminishes to a point where, statistically, it is said that on average, married couples have sex about ten times a year. That's the average. But if you were to ask them about their desire for sex, if they were to honestly introspect on their sex life, they'd tell you that the desire has not reduced. In fact, it is the same, if not more, because now, in a restricted, committed relationship, your mind thinks about sex more often.

If you were to observe it biologically, from an evolutionary point of view, continuing to search for sex at the risk of breaking a marriage is evolutionary suicide. It has significant adverse effects on your children. Continuing to desire sex can eventually break the marriage, denying your children nourishment, love, and care, and putting them through the traumatic experience of divorce and separation. However, this is exactly what happens. Evolutionarily, it does not make sense to continue to think about sex after a while, but we don't stop thinking about sex. This is because the desire for sex has nothing to do with biology or evolution. It is just one way of understanding sex.

THE MONOTONY OF MONOGAMY

There is something deeper happening in sex, something that needs to be explored and understood. Most of our explorations of the phenomenon of sex have been restricted to the bodies. We have studied human sexuality much like how we have studied human anatomy: different parts, their functionalities, and how they come together to create an experience. That is how we have tried to understand the meaning of sexual life and how it applies in a social context. There is not a single primate, other than human beings, that lives in groups - be it chimpanzees, gorillas, or any ape, our closest relatives in the animal kingdom - who practices monogamy. Not one. Chimpanzees, gorillas, bonobos - they are all polygamous. Even if we approach human sexuality biologically, there has been a narrative established that human beings are naturally monogamous and can mate for life. They can be with each other without any problems, getting all the sex they need, all the satisfaction they need, without having to worry about other partners. Now, if we were to assume this to be true, then the question arises: why do almost half of the marriages in the United States end in divorce? That's not a small number.

To say that human beings, by nature, enjoy being with one partner for life is to ignore a broader perspective. Here, in America, they have a choice; nobody is forced to get married. Unlike in India, where the majority of marriages are arranged and you may not know the compatibility, divorce is understandable - "This is not what I was searching for." In America, you know what you're looking for. You have your reasons for selecting your mate. You have your reasons for getting married, and yet, almost half of these marriages fail. Moreover, in the remaining fifty percent, the sex life is often nearly nonexistent. You are no longer interested in sex. You stay in the marriage for other reasons - social or economic reasons, children, certain commitments. All that is fine and there's nothing wrong with it, but this does not explain anything about human sexuality. When we are trying to understand why sex has become such a big problem, why it has become so perverted, and why it has disconnected Man from himself, we have to consider the institution of marriage, which is fundamentally opposed to the nature of Man as far as his sex and sexualities are concerned.

Marriage is a social contract. It is useful as an agreement, helping to bring a sense of security, rootedness, and familiarity - all of which are necessary in the modern world. For the modern man, marriage is almost a necessity. Why? Because he has already been disconnected from his clan, from his group. We have isolated Man. Here, two individuals come together, trying to satisfy each other's needs, all those needs that once took a whole village to satisfy: raising children, educating them, finding food, and protecting oneself from the harshness of the environment. All these could only be done as a group activity. Human beings could survive only when they relied on each other as part of a community. That is why, no matter how far back you go in time, you will not find one husband and one wife living alone with two kids. You cannot even imagine such an arrangement. Forget about liking that arrangement or not; you would not have even survived. The sheer burden of finding food and raising children would have completely overwhelmed your capacity, including your sex life.

If we look at human history evolutionarily, we lived as hunter-gatherers for over two million years before we began cultivating crops and became an agricultural society. We lived in small communities, ranging from about twenty individuals to about one hundred to one hundred fifty individuals. In these communities, everything was shared, including responsibilities. The community provided emotional and spiritual support. There were elders who had gone through the experiences of childbirth and life, who were there to provide guidance for the younger members. There was a great exchange of knowledge and information.

There was no necessity for marriage because you knew each and every member of that community; there were no strangers. The whole concept of tying yourself to one individual did not make any sense. It was perfectly alright to have sex with multiple partners. If you study the human sex organs, even human biology points in one direction: We are meant to have lots of sex with lots of people. Consider this: The human penis is the longest and thickest of all the apes. Compare it to chimpanzees, bonobos, gorillas, or any of the primates - it is significantly larger. Why? There is a direct correlation between promiscuity and the size of the organ. The larger the organ, the more promiscuous the species tends to be. As far as existence is concerned, the word "promiscuity" does not even make sense because we are biologically designed to have sex throughout our lives, multiple times with multiple partners, and it is the same for women.

There was a study conducted about the size of a woman's breasts. Again, human beings, compared to all other animals in existence, have some of the largest breasts. If you think about it evolutionarily, this is a big disadvantage if you are living in the wild, carrying children, and then have to walk to find food, fend for yourself, and protect yourself from predators. Large breasts can be a hindrance; they can make running and many other activities difficult. Evolutionarily, it does not make sense. And you don't need large breasts to feed your babies. Again, chimps and other apes are examples. They breastfeed without any problem, and you can hardly notice their breasts.

There are countless other animals where, unless you consciously look for breasts, you will not even see them. You will see teats and that's about it. Women have large breasts because it is a way of displaying sexuality, a way of attracting a male. It is not just an organ for the production of milk; it is a sexual organ for a woman, just like a large penis is for a man.

Biologically and evolutionarily, if you study humans in relation to other animals, you can see that we are meant to be in a group. We are meant to copulate freely, not just to reproduce, but also as a pastime, as entertainment. This was the case when we were hunter-gatherers; we didn't have to complicate sexuality. How do we know this to be true?

Even now, if you study the remnants of ancient civilizations, people who have not become overly civilized in the traditional sense - who don't live in big cities, who don't work in concrete jungles, who still live close to the earth, whose lifestyle is still very natural - you will find that almost all these communities practice polygamy. Even in communities where marriage exists as a ritual, there are times during the year when the marriage contract is temporarily suspended so that people can come together and have sex. For the rest of the time, they are married and know who their partner is, but the contract is suspended. Why? Because they understand the spiritual necessity of sex, the spiritual nourishment that sex provides through another body, another mind, another touch, another language.

What is sex on the outside if not the language of the body? It is one of our basic communication tools. Without the use of any sophisticated language, a human being can use his or her body to express all their emotions, all their feelings. It's a communication tool. Polygamy encourages more communication, more interaction, and more nourishment. That is why sex remained pure and pristine in small human communities. You will not hear of sexually motivated crimes or aggression in sex. These things don't even enter their minds because they live in a community. The value of a community is so grossly underestimated that humanity has yet to realize that this lack of community is one of the biggest causes of all our social problems. While we identify ourselves as part of the human community and use the word "community" - we have figured out different ways of keeping in touch with each other - but at the individual level, at the fundamental level where it matters, we have become isolated. We have separated ourselves from all that was meant to nourish us. We have become detached from the source of great nourishment; our fellow human beings, the people around us.

When Man first began cultivating crops, in one sense he gave birth to an era of abundance. He could produce his own crops, preserve them, and didn't need to run around to hunt and gather. In one sense, this was useful. But in another sense, it is said that our shift from being hunter-gatherers to farmers was the biggest fall from which Man has never recovered. Many of the modern diseases can be traced back to an agricultural lifestyle. Before this transition, diseases like smallpox, measles, and diarrhea were not recorded. They spread in human communities where too many people lived together in a small area, not just one hundred or one hundred fifty people, but thousands living together. It is said this is where we started our downhill journey.

Firstly, our nutritional needs were not fully met by agriculture because when you are hunting and gathering, you can supplement your diet with everything necessary. Nothing is restricting you. You can eat an animal, fruits, nuts, and berries. And because you're hunting and gathering, your body naturally moves towards the things it lacks, naturally supplementing itself. However, in agriculture, there is a limitation as to what and how much you can produce. Agriculture is more conducive to producing one type of grain as opposed to many varieties. That is why even now, almost ninety percent of our agricultural produce is made up of corn, rice, wheat, millet, and barley. These grains don't supply us with all the nutrients we need - that's why we need meat, that's why we need fruits and vegetables. But now we live in a world where we have perfected exchange. We don't have to produce everything we need by ourselves. Whatever we can produce, we produce; the rest we obtain from elsewhere. But imagine during the early stages of farming, without technology, and without transportation, you simply ate what you grew. Naturally, your physical vitality was reduced.

From there began all that we now recognize as problematic for sex: the class division. One group of people became farmers, working in the fields, and growing crops. Then another class emerged, one that simply lived off this produce. They didn't have to create anything or move from place to place; all they had to do was tax these people. A new class of society began to emerge: the ruling class. You cannot even imagine a ruling class in a community of hunter-gatherers where everybody is equally involved in activities. The moment you create a divide between human beings, the moment you introduce this artificial separation, you have introduced a great divide, which will only continue to widen to a point where this division has fully isolated an individual, stripped him of all his basic connections, his desire to be with multiple people, and his desire to share his love and happiness with many because you have isolated him for selfish reasons. Marriage becomes an indispensable institution for the ruling class because you cannot control a nomadic tribe. But you can easily control someone who's committed, who is bound, who has private property. He cannot simply move around. What we think of as advancement - moving from being hunter-gatherers to farmers and creating what we now recognize as civilization - is actually a downfall. We lived freely, openly, in an environment that was perfectly conducive for sex. Our bodies were perfectly adapted to the environment, and our minds were perfectly tuned for that type of relationship.

That change is what destroyed our pure understanding of sex. Why is there so much perversion in sex? Why is it condemned on the one hand by religious groups, yet on the other hand, it thrives as an industry? In America, pornography is one of the fastest-growing industries, a hundred-billion-dollar industry. So much for a culture that does not like to talk about sex. We have become liars, cheaters, and hypocrites because of this divide. Because we have fashioned our lives based on our own arbitrary rules of social interaction and exchange, we have tried to fit sex into that mold, but sex is too great a phenomenon to fit into our social structures. Yes, we have popularized marriage, but we have not removed the terrors of living by denying our sexuality. That is why we have found as many different ways as possible to express our sexuality. That is why sex is everywhere: in our books, in our movies, in our language. Many curse words are sexual - yet, when you are scolding someone, what is the necessity to bring in sex?

Because our understanding of sex is so limited and restrictive, we are baffled. With so much sophistication and understanding of life around us, with all our scientific discoveries and inventions, why haven't we created more happiness in the world? Why haven't we fostered more joy, more contentment? It's because we have not understood sex - the biggest force contributing to our emotions, the only thing that can give meaning to our lives. If that is not understood, then what is the use of all our sophistication? That is why humanity only appears to be sophisticated, only appears to be civilized. It's all superficial.

Enter the substructures, look into the families, go into individual lives, and you will see that individuals are suffering. They are stressed out. Statistics clearly show this. More people now are stressed, anxious, worried, suicidal, and depressed than ever before in human history, and this is despite our so-called civilized, advanced status. Why? Because we have not understood the primary force. We have not explored the actual act of sex or the actual meaning of sex. We have not recognized it as a spiritual activity, an answer to our questions, or a way to be happy, content, and blissful. We have only viewed it as a deviation from our regular activities - a pleasure to be restricted so that human beings can view themselves as workers, not as creators. It is a great ploy of society, of the ruling class. It is the narrative set by them, because the moment you start exploring sex your whole understanding of life changes. You will not see yourself merely as an animal that has to work from morning to evening.

Modern man works longer than all his predecessors. While we view the hunting and gathering lifestyle as primitive, they actually had a lot more time on their hands. After finishing their hunting and gathering, it is said that they used to sleep for about four hours during the day, apart from a full, comfortable sleep at night. They had so much time they didn't know what to do with it. They started creating things. If you look at many of our prized creations - clothing, utensils, tools used for knitting, sewing - these were invented during our hunting-gathering phase. They are not recent inventions. Creativity flourished at that time because there was time.

Now, what is modern man mostly engaged in? He is struggling to survive. He has no time for himself. Naturally, the way he approaches sex changes. The only way to go beyond this deep, traumatic past of ours and to rediscover our playfulness is to rewrite the definition of sex, to relook at everything we know about sex. We have to approach it not physically, biologically, or socially, but spiritually.

Orgasm

The Harem Fantasy

Why do men fantasize about having a harem of women to have sex with? Why do women not have the same fantasy?

First, a story. There's a story that is told about President Calvin Coolidge and a chicken farm. This is a popular story, but let me share it anyway.

The President and his wife were visiting a commercial chicken farm in the 1920s. During the tour, the First Lady asked the farmer how he managed to produce so many fertile eggs with only a few roosters. The farmer proudly explained that his roosters happily performed their duty dozens of times each day. "Perhaps, you could mention that to the President," replied the first lady. Overhearing the remark, President Coolidge asked the farmer, "Does each cock service the same hen each time?" "Oh no," replied the farmer. "He always changes from one hen to another." "I see, replied the President. Perhaps you could point that out to Mrs. Coolidge."

Both men and women fantasize. Let us try and understand what a fantasy is. In sex, it is not simple imagination. It is something more. While the word "fantasy" comes from Greek "phantasia" to mean imagination, literally to visualize, to see things, fantasies in sex have a deeper personality. There is structure to it. There is a pattern to it. And more often than not, it is opposed to the patterns and structures that you have accepted on the outside. That is why it is hard to reconcile who you are as a person on the outside and what you fantasize about. More often than not, you fantasize in a way that you're not. You fantasize about things that you don't experience. If you go a little deeper and understand the psychology of fantasizing, the entire purpose of it is to express your repressed self.

Once we understand how common repression is and how deep repression goes, we can easily understand the sheer variety of fantasies. We don't have to go inside the mind of a man or the mind of a woman to see what their fantasies are. You can get an insight into their fantasies just by understanding their impressions. Men and women are repressed differently, but both are repressed - that is why they rely on fantasizing. Otherwise, there is no need for sex to occupy the mind. There is no need to create complex role plays. There's no need for sex to be attached to emotions and behaviors. The very fact that sex is more entertaining, more engaging, and more thrilling when it has a story attached to it, when it has a narrative to follow, says that we are playing out are repressed emotions in our fantasies.

IMAGINATION VS. REALITY

Let's begin with men. Your question is, "Why do men fantasize about having a harem of women to have sex with?" It's because they actually cannot satisfy a harem of women. In reality - biologically and physically - it is impossible. Firstly, the time he takes to become aroused, to get into the mood, and how quickly he finishes makes it hard for him to satisfy even one woman without changing some of his regular sexual patterns. His fear in the real world, is finishing off too quickly. That is man's biggest frustration. He's all excited. He has great fantasies in his mind, great desires. He also puts in enormous effort to get the sex he wants. His whole life is an effort directed towards getting that sex. He could have put in years of work in getting richer, becoming smarter, in moving towards a particular woman, but when he is allowed to experience the pleasure, to get the rewards of all his efforts it's all over in ten minutes - tops. More often than not, in five minutes he's done. That's his frustration.

In fantasies, he can have sex for a long time, for hours together, satisfying multiple women. That is his fantasy. That is his imagination. Once in a while, he might actually get an opportunity to physically be with multiple women. But still, he knows the moment he drops from the realm of imagination, his sexuality does not allow the fantasy of being with and actually enjoying being with multiple women. That disconnection is what we see in man's fantasies. That is why he talks about it a lot because, for him, the actual act of sex is so brief. The satisfaction is so limited. There's always something that is missing in his sexual experience. If you notice, very rarely is a man satisfied with his sexual experiences. He knows that there is a gap between the way he has approached sex and the way he wants to. That manifests itself in the imagination.

But for a woman, it's a different matter altogether. Firstly, the question, why do women not have the same fantasy? They do have such fantasies. I'll share one example. In "Mating in Captivity," Esther Perel shares a story of one of her clients. She says,

"When Catherine hit puberty, she was fifty pounds overweight, sexually invisible, repeatedly rejected, she was the "ugly sidekick" left guarding the door while her girlfriends made out on the other side of it. Today, she's a beautiful woman, married for almost fifteen years. She and her husband play out a fantasy in which she is a high-priced prostitute. Men pay top dollar for the pleasure of her

company. They want her so much they're willing to spend a small fortune and risk their jobs and marriages for a little bit of her time. The more outrageous their transgressions, the greater her value. Catherine's past humiliations are vindicated by the men who now can't walk past her without marveling. In her theater of the surreal, she triumphantly exacts revenge for the pains and frustrations of her adolescence."

She also gives another example of a woman who fantasizes about having sex with cowboys, pirates, kings, and concubines, as they parade in endless configurations of carefully wielded power and highly refined surrender. What is the necessity for a woman to fantasize about being with multiple men? And also if you observe these examples, there is a structure to it. There is an underlying emotional structure. For a man, a sexual fantasy is a way of expressing himself. It's a way of communication. Why? Because man is not allowed to share his thoughts. That is his biggest problem, and that is the biggest suppression - he's supposed to be a man. By the very definition, he cannot be sensitive, he cannot share what's happening inside. He cannot be vulnerable.

What happens to all these emotions that are a part of his childhood? During his growing years, he was obviously vulnerable and sensitive. He had his fears, frustrations, and had taken insults. Now, what would happen to all these when the body becomes so rigid that you don't use it as an avenue to express these emotions? The body has a natural way of throwing things out. While anger looks like a deviation from the normal emotional state, it is actually catharsis. When a man is angry, when he's screaming, shouting, and when his body is moving in a certain way, something is releasing inside. At least briefly for that moment, he's able to throw it out. Now, what happens when you are not given an opportunity to throw your anger or your frustrations out? What if you have to maintain a certain image for hours every day, and the moment you step out of the house, you cannot be yourself? You have to leave that child behind. You have to leave the insecurities behind. You have to become something totally different.

Public vs. Private

The body begins to accumulate all these repressions. It is said that in sex, man expresses himself sometimes in a way that seems like it is not his nature. Sometimes he's more aggressive in sex than necessary; he's more dominant than necessary. Why? Because sex is the only such activity where you can safely lose control. He chooses sex as his way of losing control. Now, this is important to understand both for men as well as women. There is no use in complaining that your man is something different in bed and outside. You married a nice gentleman - a soft spoken, delicate, wonderful individual. And in the night, he wants to handcuff you. How would you reconcile with this? This is where a lot of conflicts arise. When two individuals start talking about sex, and talking about making it interesting, their personalities are totally different. This makes you question your choice: Did I marry the soft-spoken gentleman or the one who handcuffs me? Who is real? Neither is real. Your man is something totally different. Your woman is something totally different. You cannot judge them based on how they behave when they're around people and how they behave in sex because these are two extremes. In the world, they are not at all their true selves. So if you see a soft-spoken gentleman, all the qualities that you have fallen in love with, but in private, if he's a little more raw, if he is a little more unpolished, unkempt, there is a conflict. There's no way you can assume that the way a man is presenting himself is who he is.

No man is the same because we are living in an unnatural setup. We are living in a structured prison-like environment where we have to watch what we do and say, because there are repercussions in the world. In a way, the world is vast, but it's a very big prison. How do we know that it's a prison? Try being yourself for a single moment. See if that pure expression of freedom doesn't go unpunished. People will notice. People will criticize. People will question. That's what you're scared of more often than not. It's not just the law, it's the immediate reaction of people. That is why you walk, talk, and dress a certain way; although, deep down you're nothing like that. Similarly, in sex, it is the other extreme. He is role playing. He is freely using his body to communicate, to throw things out. If he wants to feel dominant, you can see that behavior in sex. Now, that is why if you observe sexual fantasies that are played out in what we recognize as purely artificial setups - it could be a movie, it could be porn - you will see that the fantasies are extreme. They're not normal. Which makes us question, are we the same people?

In real life, we won't even talk about these things. We don't even think like this, but we love watching it. We enjoy it. All those qualities that we actually don't like, we like it in sex. We don't like violence in real life. We are not violent when we are going about a natural life. But look at the expression violence finds in sex. Rape is a direct result of one idiot trying to express his dominance in a totally uncontrolled way with no regard for another body. Such a thing is possible because repression is there. Why don't we hear about rapes in the wild? Of course, if you dig deeper, if you actually want to find it, you will find a few examples, but even there, you will hardly find violence. Rarely in nature are sex and violence connected. Why? Because nobody is suppressing them. There is no false identity to satisfy. They're not dealing with pent-up emotions. They're not dealing with abuse - physical, emotional, or social. They are free.

That is why it is hard to understand a man's fantasy, his narrative of what sex is, and that is why it is also easy to understand why he gets easily bored after a while, living with the same partner. Because he's been fantasizing about all these things, once he's married, once he is done playing out a few fantasies and then the responsibility of a family life hits, the fantasy is over. Once your partner is seen as a family member, someone you love, someone you care for, you cannot fantasize the same way. There is a conflict.

There's another beautiful example Ester shares. She says:

There's this woman who loves watching her husband perform on stage. He's a musician. She says "I'm immediately aroused when I'm sitting and watching him perform - just the way he moves, the way he sings, the way he handles his instruments. I'm sitting there and having all these fantasies." And then she asks her, "Do you ever go to the bathroom after he steps down from the stage, do you guys go in for a quick experience?" She says, "No." And then she asks her "Why not? I mean, it's like there he is exactly the way you like him. Freely expressing himself, and you're all aroused, then what happens?" She says "the moment he steps down from the stage I am immediately de-aroused. And by the time we get back home, I have no interest because he is him. He's no longer that person who's on the stage. He's my husband." So she says, "well, why don't you divorce him? It's like you divorce him, but still be with him. Now because you're not married, you might get aroused." And she says, "you know, this is what I told him. That if you divorce me, immediately I'll be attracted to you again."

Look what she's saying. It's the same person. Nothing has changed. Just that at the moment when there is no attachment, there is no bondage, you don't own that other individual and they don't own you - what happens there? In that moment, you can play out your fantasies. Relationships struggle because there is a conflict between fantasy and reality. Initially, a relationship is almost ninety percent fantasy and ten percent reality. You don't even think about reality. You keep pushing it aside. You're only fantasizing. Every time you think about the woman, you're fantasizing. Every time the woman is thinking about the man, she's fantasizing. But slowly, reality starts creeping in - washing, cleaning, cooking, taking care of the kids - all that and the familiarity being built.

After a while, the only way they can have sex is if they're imagining about someone else. For a man, it is a way of communication. It's a way of expressing himself. For him, the sex is good when he's able to play out all his repressed emotions. That is why it's never good for him because there's no way any woman can allow him to play out all his repressions - a repression that has been accumulated over a lifetime. She'll say, "Hold on. These things are allowed. These things are not allowed. Yes, you are fantasizing, but I'm a real person."

That's one of the reasons, if you go back in time, women were suppressed. Women's sexuality was suppressed. Their voice was suppressed so that a man could simply use a woman as a way of expressing himself. He didn't want a counter-argument. He didn't want opposition. He has also arranged society in a way that he can have control - he can have control over the resources, he can have control over the freedom that he can give to a woman, and he can have control over the basic things she longs for. That acts as a bargaining tool for him to get what he wants. This won't work going forward. Women have begun to assert themselves. they've begun to assert their individuality. It is only now that we are beginning to see the fantasies of women that were hidden for so long.

Orgasm

Sensual Meditation

What are some specific techniques to turn sex into a form of meditation to grow spiritually?

Before understanding how to approach sex, it is important to understand what sex truly is. Like many things in life, we often settle for explanations that are popular rather than profound. We don't dig deeper to understand the complexities. We're so busy moving about that we overlook things very close to us - things that could answer many of our questions. Because we are in a hurry, we accept superficial explanations and ideas that are easy to understand and simple to apply. Anything profound that requires a bit of involvement is often ignored. This is how sex has remained a mystery for such a long time. It's not that we are far removed from sex or that we don't know what sex is, but everything we know about it comes from superficial understanding, from observations from the outside.

The only way to truly understand what sex is, is to see what it does to you, what happens on the inside. When there are no images, no imagination, no faults -

if you were to connect with sex as a state of being, not as an act, you would see that sex is something totally different from the general explanations of it. Our understanding of sex is nowhere near encompassing the totality of what sex is. Sex is so deep; it goes to the very source of things. It addresses the fundamental problems of life: pain, suffering, unawareness, unconsciousness, and discontentment - sex illuminates every single dimension of life. There is not a part of life that sex doesn't touch. Yet, in the realm of explanations, it remains limited.

SEX IS INSIDE

While we can see the sheer magnanimity and universality of sex - how every single living thing in existence is bound by it, lives and dies within it - our explanations are limited to pleasure and reproduction. It is restricted to the body. We are so obsessed with the body that all our explanations of sex are also confined to it. So, before we dive into techniques and methods, we must first understand sex itself. More importantly, we have to step away from all borrowed notions of what sex is. You have to redefine sex for yourself. Everything must be defined from your perspective. What happens to your emotions during sex? What happens to your desires, your self-identity, and your fears during sex? These must be defined by you, independent of the worldly explanations of what sex is. That is the starting point for understanding a phenomenon as transcendental and significant as sex.

Now, where can you begin? You cannot begin from the outside because the moment you see yourself in the act of sex, you are observing from the outside. You have become the observer. Everything understood from the outside is useless for truly understanding sex. From the inside, how you experience sex matters, not how you view it. Your opinions and judgments don't matter. The moment you drop this desire to observe sex from the outside - all the emphasis on different positions, different ways of having sex, the kind of partner you're going to find, the kind of environment you will be having sex in, whether by candlelight, in bright daylight, or in a completely dark room - none of it matters. It's only a basic setup; it might help you set the right mood. Once you understand internally what you're trying to experience, then you can adjust the external to suit that.

Your understanding of sex from the inside determines the place and the mood on the outside, so there's no need to get overly concerned with the physicality of sex. Unfortunately, almost all discussions on sex - how to improve your sex life, how to get the best out of sex, how to satisfy yourself and your partner - are connected to this one simple dimension: observation from the outside. It's more about how sex looks. But does it really matter how it looks? You are trying to understand what's happening on the inside. You are using it as a tool for self-transformation. You're not trying to transform the way you look. You're not trying to satisfy the ego. You're not even trying to satisfy your partner. Here, the entire emphasis is on your self-transformation. Of course, when self-transformation becomes the center of sex, you eventually involve your partner. Two individuals can come together mutually to help each other connect with themselves better and to grow spiritually. This is a totally different approach to sex.

Sex as pleasure, reproduction, fun, or play are all distinct; but sex as a spiritual practice is something entirely different. You cannot approach sex in the same way. You cannot approach it as a means of getting something. You cannot approach it with an end goal in mind. The biggest difference between sex as a desire and sex as a spiritual practice is that in sex as a desire, you know what the goal is. Your mind is fully occupied with the thought of reaching that goal. Imagine if I were to tell you that you can have sex but you cannot have an orgasm - there is no such thing as orgasm. Would you still be interested in sex as a desire? Not at all. The entire enchantment and allure of sex falls away immediately because what is it that you are doing? Observe how people have sex, observe how we have defined sex. It is all goal-oriented because there is an orgasm at the end of it. Because you know it's an experience that you enjoy, you go through the motions of sex, and you put in all the effort to eventually reach that destination. If you want to approach sex as a spiritual practice, the first thing you need to drop is a goal because the very act of sex, every moment of it, should be transformed into an orgasmic experience. This requires a bit of understanding.

In what we recognize as normal sex, the pleasure is in the end. The pleasure that you're deriving in the process is only coming from a reflection of the pleasure that you're moving towards. That is why if you look at a man immediately after orgasm, something changes. He has no interest in sex. He has no interest in doing all the things he was doing just one second before. What happened? If he was deriving pleasure in the activity of sex, then why did he suddenly stop? He was not deriving pleasure in the activity. He was deriving pleasure in the idea that he was moving towards orgasm. It is the same for a woman, but because a woman can have multiple orgasms, it is harder to see this. Even she is moving towards orgasm. If you take away orgasm, she would also lose interest in sex.

To transform sex into meditation, you should look for the pleasure of orgasm right here and now, with one difference: it does not matter the depth of it, nor how satisfying it is. There is no need to compare the pleasure that you're seeking in the activity to the ultimate - of course, orgasm will always triumph in terms of sheer exhilaration, but that is part of the process because you're only beginning to understand sex. You are learning to use it as a technique. Initially, it might seem futile because you're not moving towards orgasm. You're trying to find nothing. You are in a state of surrender, acceptance, observation, and awareness. All these things can only happen in the present moment.

Why is there a connection between sex and meditation? How can we even equate the two? In both meditation and sex, you are present. That is the common connection. When you're sitting still, when you're closing your eyes, irrespective of what you're watching, there is a watcher. It's undeniable. And eventually becoming that watcher is the destination of meditation. It's exactly the same in sex. There is a watcher. He is watching the act, the movement, the changing emotions, and the changes happening in the inner landscape. Now, if you can become that watcher, if you can shift from the activity to the one who is enjoying the activity, you become fully rooted in the present moment. The moment you become rooted in the present moment, you have opened the door. You've opened the pathway. You have figured out the method, the technique. Once you learn how to be in the present moment in sex, half your work is done. That is the biggest challenge, because the generally accepted idea of sex is that you should forget yourself. Otherwise, how can you do all those things? Somewhere because you are forgetting yourself, you're forgetting who you are, and you give yourself the license to do all the things that you do.

The challenge of turning sex into a spiritual practice is that you must engage in all those actions consciously. Kissing, hugging, and embracing must all be conscious. Every single moment must be experienced without any desire to go anywhere. In fact, your sex should become play. In play, you're not aiming to reach a destination; the objective of play is simply to play. Similarly, sex should become like a dance - you dance to dance, not to reach somewhere. Sex should transform into an art form, an expression, a moment of creativity. It should become an act for the sake of that act alone, not for anything beyond it. The technique begins with cultivating a mindset of not seeking anything in sex. This changes the quality of sex completely. The way you approach it changes, what you do there changes. All the issues of not connecting with your partner, not respecting your partner, and not understanding your partner, all these things will automatically fall into place.

If two individuals come together without knowing why they have come together, the moment they stop seeking in sex, the moment they let go of craving in sex, their minds and egos fall away. So, too, do all their fantasies, imaginations, repressions, desires to dominate, and desires to control. Right then and there, sex becomes spiritual.

It is still a play. You are still engaging playfully with the idea of each other's bodies. You are still children, but there is no society, no world, no one watching, and no one judging because remember, you are the world. There is no world out there. Close your eyes - where is the world? It's inside you. All the judgment, all the guilt, all the fear of the world hides in you, in your mind. And that is what you have been bringing to sex. To turn sex into a spiritual exercise, you must drop the world. The easiest, the simplest way to drop the world is to drop your mind. There is nothing more beautiful in existence than to see two bodies in communion where the mind is absent. That sex is pure. It is divine. It is transcendental because there are no rules. It is natural, what the body is doing there, because you are so aware of what's happening. Awareness completely transforms the quality of sex. You can't be in a hurry when you're aware. You cannot be angry when you're aware. You cannot be egoistic when you're aware. Awareness itself is divine. You are connecting with pure consciousness.

Intercourse

Now, what happens when two such pure entities meet, when two individuals learn how to set their minds aside? This won't happen immediately; it's what you are moving towards. But if you can set your mind aside and then meet, you will truly meet for the first time. Intercourse happens because there are not two separate consciousnesses or awarenesses. Awareness is one, consciousness is one. It appears reflected in us separately because we have independent bodies and minds. But in the act of sex, the illusions of the mind and body drop. It is the meeting of two consciousnesses that had previously assumed they were separate - a consciousness that was artificially divided by the body. And now there is a pure merger, and that is why the term "intercourse" exists.

Think about it: why is it not called "outercourse"? Because the merger has to happen inside. But how do we normally approach sex? Most people, while using the word "intercourse," are only having "outercourse." They are only merging at the level of the body. They never go inside. They never connect with themselves. How can you have intercourse when you are not inside? The most important question you need to ask during sex is, "Am I inside, or am I outside?" If you are outside, then you're not having intercourse. You're having outercourse. Suddenly, without your knowledge, without your awareness, in a single moment, intercourse happens accidentally. That is what you recognize as orgasm. And that again happens independently of your partner. You climax on your own; she climaxes on her own. That is the closest you come to intercourse. But even then, there is no real intercourse happening because you both have not come together. The merger has not happened. One of you is dissatisfied. One of you is still longing for the merger. That is why I say most sex is simply an outercourse. It is only in spiritual sex that you experience true intercourse.

This word is beautiful and requires a bit of understanding: "inter" doesn't just mean inside; it also means in between. Just like when we discuss space, we can talk about the inside, the outside, and the interspace - the space in between that we cannot see or touch, yet it exists. What you are trying to experience is that space within the space that you are occupying. Your body occupies a certain space, and so does your partner's. Now, what are you trying to do? Why are you moving around so much? What are you trying to connect to? If you observe, you're trying to connect to a space within the visible space. That is why we call it intercourse, where you literally split open space itself and connect with something inner. That is why the word "sex" literally means to divide. Sex is not a union; it's a division. It's a way of breaking open.

If you observe two people having sex, it's almost like you've given them a box filled with treasure that's locked, handed them the key, and turned off the light. Now, whatever you hear, whatever you recognize, is them trying to open that box. Sometimes the box falls, and they pick it up; they can't see it. Sometimes they're trying to open it from the wrong end. However you want to imagine it, sometimes they don't even know they're supposed to open it. They're doing all kinds of things to that box, but eventually, they stumble, find the keyhole, and the key. Unconsciously, the key goes into the lock, and it opens. And then they black out. That's an orgasm. This is what sex is.

If you want to turn this process into a spiritual process, you must bring light into the room. Sex cannot be in darkness. It must occur under the broad daylight of your consciousness, with full awareness and acceptance under the glorious witness of your consciousness. Initially, it might seem ridiculous because you've always had sex in the dark. Now, for the first time, you are actually seeing what you're doing. You see how silly it looks, how awkward it seems, but you must persist. You must watch it until you realize that the entire process of conscious sex is to connect with that interspace that exists between the spaces you both occupy. If that is the objective, then how you approach sex changes because it is not about reaching a destination; that space is not somewhere far away.

Wherever there is space, there is an interspace. That is why pleasure is within you. With just a little bit of movement, a little arrangement of your body, some action or inaction, you can touch that pleasure center. Why? Because the center is everywhere. It's not somewhere outside; you don't have to depend on something external. It's just that because you haven't approached it directly, your mind has become conditioned to believe that sex has meaning only when it happens in a certain way, when you perform certain actions, and when you are with someone else. These ideas are fixed in your mind.

Now, how do you see the parallel between this and meditation? What happens in meditation? Initially, you struggle with your mind, you wrestle with your body. But eventually, you settle down, you sink deeper, and you relax. Ultimately, what are you trying to experience in meditation? You are trying to enter that interspace where the disturbances of the mind and body are nonexistent, where you exist as a pure being, without pain, without suffering. The weight of the body is gone, the heat of the body is gone, the pressure is gone. All that you recognize as your body, which is nothing but sensations of discomfort, disappears. You cannot even imagine what pure aliveness is - aliveness without any strain, stress, or desire. That's what you're craving, but that is nothing but the interspace that lies between everything that you observe. You are just trying to connect with it.

You're doing the same in sex; you're trying to connect with that space. In sex, you are using the natural affinity towards sex, the natural craving, and the natural desire, all of which are already inbuilt, already programmed inside you. You're actually using these to trick yourself into awakening. You might like or dislike meditation, depending on whether the conditioning has set in or not. But there is no question of not liking sex. The conditioning is already there. Now, isn't it intelligent, isn't it smart, to use something in which you've already invested so much energy? To use something that already has a set pattern leading you all the way to orgasm?

The Orgasm of Enlightenment

The orgasm you experience in sex and enlightenment are not two different things. The only difference is that in sex, the orgasm is accidental - it just happens. You don't know why it happened. You don't know how it happened, so you cannot replicate it on your own. You have to go through that process again. But in meditation, once you touch that zone, you can stay there as long as you want. That's the biggest difference. The nature of the bliss is exactly the same. Every time you experience an orgasm, you are actually experiencing a mini-enlightenment. It is enlightenment, but what you want is to hold on to it. You don't want to lose it.

The moment you understand that orgasm is nothing but an enlightenment that you're unable to hold onto, you can reevaluate sex. "Let me approach sex in such a way that I move towards it slowly, gradually, one step at a time, in such a way that when I find it, when the ultimate explosion happens, I can actually hold on to it because I have moved consciously." In regular sex, you blindly dash towards orgasm. That is why it lasts only for as long as it does. In sex, as a spiritual exercise, you take your time. You slow down. You become conscious. You become aware. You don't look for the orgasm. You look for the feeling of orgasm, the experience of orgasm, in everything you're doing. Your touch should be an orgasm. Your kiss should be an orgasm. Your embrace should be an orgasm. There is no need to crave the end.

If you approach sex consciously, it is only a matter of time before you understand the realm you are in so much that a single touch takes you to ecstasy. You don't need all the imagination. You don't need to strain your body. You don't need to stress your body. Just a single touch - because that is how close orgasm is to you. It is not far away. You have created a distance. You have artificially pushed it away because you have created an arbitrary structure to get to it, and you enjoy that structure. You find the struggle in that structure fascinating. You can't understand the idea of experiencing orgasm without any work, without any effort.

It almost seems unfair that while the whole world struggles to touch that interspace, once you understand it, you can connect with it almost effortlessly. Well, that's what spirituality is about. That's the essence of moving in a certain direction, what meditation teaches: not to focus solely on the ultimate experience, but to progress in the right direction. This connection between sex and spirituality isn't something new. It's only in the past few centuries that we've condemned sex and relegated it to the corner.

There was a time when sex held a central place in spirituality. For instance, there's a temple in Madhya Pradesh, India, called Khajuraho. This temple is unique because its entire complex is adorned with rock carvings depicting people, their lifestyles, and a variety of activities. More than ten percent of all statues are dedicated to displaying sex in an array of positions, in ways that our modern imagination cannot match in creativity. Consider how fearlessly and openly these are displayed on the temple walls. Temples are considered the most sacred spaces, places of divinity. You don't enter a temple unclean, nor do you enter demanding favors or carrying your ego. You enter to surrender, to transform, to merge with something greater. The temple is a sacred space, and here on its walls, people are depicted having sex.

It is said that the Khajuraho Temple served as a meditation school. Before entering the temple, initiates were required to sit outside and contemplate sex. This was because the first obstacle to overcome is one's obsession with sex, the misunderstandings about it, and the unawareness of its divinity. You sit there, think about it, imagine it, and try to understand it deeply. Only when your understanding of sex deepens and matures are you allowed to enter the temple. Just imagine if the walls of the Vatican were adorned with figures of people having sex. The issue arises when we choose to suppress something we don't understand, pushing it away instead of connecting it with something higher, something deeper.

The church never talks about sex as a way of transcendence. It never talks about sex as a way of connecting with that ultimate bliss that you're searching for. It never says what you're searching for is within you because that is not the business of the church. It is an institution which is engaged in something entirely different. It has nothing to do with orgasm. It has nothing to do with bliss. It has nothing to do with you. It has everything to do with something else. But if you go back to ancient cultures, you will see sex was at the center. The yogic practice of tantra is all about using your body to connect with your partner's body in a meditative way, in silence, in stillness, to become enlightened. Tantra is a complete technique of enlightenment using sex alone.

Let me share a couple of techniques you can use. One tantric method is all about watchfulness, about aligning your breath, your internal emotions, and the physical sensations all together through awareness. In tantra, you focus entirely on what's happening inside. Sometimes you're aware of your body sensations; other times, you connect with the surging emotions within. Occasionally, you connect with inner stillness and silence, but none of these aspects have a form.

Consider the meaning of "tantra": it literally involves using the body as a technique of meditation, yet you're not consciously thinking about or visualizing the body.

Another technique involves embracing the duality of your experiences. Life is inherently dualistic; everything you experience comes in pairs. In sex, there's action and stillness, noise and silence - all internal. To deepen your sexual experience spiritually, you can alternate between these opposites. For instance, in typical sex, which is not spiritually oriented, movement is random - there's no rhythm, awareness, or pause; it's uncontrolled. However, in spiritual sex, you move consciously and then pause. During this pause, you relax deeply, then move again. This mirrors what you do in meditation but with your partner's help. You and your partner can help each other alternate between activity and stillness, tension and relaxation. Feel and recognize the moments of stress in your body, and when it peaks, relax together. This coordination soon becomes intuitive. Understanding that the goal of sex is to connect with silence and stillness here and now means that when one partner becomes silent, the other follows naturally. Observing this process externally, it resembles playing a musical instrument or engaging in a dance.

What is the difference between dance and just chaotic movement? In dance, there is pause, rhythm, watchfulness, and observation. In chaotic movement, each person does what they want. There's no rhythm because there's no synchronized pause. When you synchronize your pauses, you transform a simple act of moving into a spiritual exercise. Similarly, you can move between imagination and emptiness. Though you aim to keep your mind out, there will be moments when it's challenging. The mind intrudes. You want to see what's happening; you want to imagine it. Allow some space for that, especially initially, when you are learning to set the mind aside. Dedicate some time for imagination but turn that into a meditation too. Imagine together. Then stop simultaneously. Coordinate imagination as well as emptiness. Imagine intensely, and when it reaches a peak, coordinate using time - initially use something external, but eventually, you'll intuitively know when to stop. For example, if you're imagining for five minutes intensely, you'll sense when your partner stops as something changes in the body, and you should also stop. Alternate between imagination and emptiness, and between excitement and relaxation. Let your body and mind reach peaks of excitement, then relax. During relaxation, connect with the common stillness you both experience.

That is what distinguishes a simple meditation from sex. In sex, two people can support each other. You can become each other's cues, triggers, and pathways. When you forget to do something, if your partner remembers, it helps bring you back. If you forget to relax, and your partner relaxes, it reminds you to do the same. It's harder to forget when two people are trying to remember the same thing. That is why sex has always been regarded as a high form of meditation - one of the highest forms - because two individuals are trying to connect with the same thing and help each other. For instance, if you feel sleepy during meditation, there's nobody to prevent you from falling asleep. But try falling asleep during sex; the consequences will indeed be dire. So, you remain engaged, driven by the natural fascination with sex that keeps you awake and alert to the process.

Many challenges in meditation subside naturally in sex; you only need to introduce some structure to it. Yes, it may seem chaotic, but it's a structured chaos. Eventually, you will find your rhythm and begin to devise your own techniques. There's no need to learn many different methods because once you grasp the basic principle of what you are aiming to connect with, you will naturally invent ways to achieve it.

This understanding of sex differs significantly from the worldly understanding. Unfortunately, for most of the human race, sex is merely a means of releasing internal stress - a momentary pleasure that is biological rather than spiritual or divine. However, as an individual, you have the power to transform sex into a comprehensive method, a complete technique that can elevate you from unconsciousness to consciousness, from bondage to freedom.

In "Letters from the Earth" Mark Twain says,

Man has imagined a heaven, and has left entirely out of it the supremest of all his delights, the one ecstasy that stands first and foremost in the heart of every individual of his race -- and of ours -- sexual intercourse!

It is as if a lost and perishing person in a roasting desert should be told by a rescuer he might choose and have all longed-for things but one, and he should elect to leave out water!

Orgasm is a door. It is the grandest of doors, and there is only one key that can unlock it permanently. Consciousness. Watchfulness in sex is a direct path to enlightenment.

Orgasm

About Nirvana

Originally from India, our teacher, Nirvana, embarked on his professional journey in the corporate sector shortly after completing his college education. However, at the age of 24, he realized there was a deep void within him that material achievements could not fill. Yearning for inner tranquility and a sense of purpose, he made the courageous decision to move away from home, leave his job, rent a modest room, and dedicate himself to the pursuit of meditation.

Devoting several years to intense meditation, Nirvana experienced a profound spiritual awakening that forever transformed his life. Motivated by this newfound understanding, he eagerly began sharing his experiences through various programs and retreats. In 2017, he traveled to the United States with one of his students, and upon arrival, he intuitively knew he had found the right place to sow the seeds of consciousness and awareness.

Nirvana Foundation is a nonprofit organization dedicated to providing individuals with opportunities to explore meditation and self-awareness through books and programs. Nirvana speaks twice a day, and his talks are recorded and transcribed by his students. These transcripts are ultimately compiled into books for publication. Currently, our teacher resides and teaches in Tennessee, where the development of the first Nirvana meditation retreat is underway.

Share Your Thoughts

If this book has touched your life, illuminated your path, or opened new avenues of thought and introspection, consider sharing your experience. Your review on Amazon will help us reach others who are searching for answers. Your reflections, insights, and experiences can light the way for fellow seekers on the path to Awakening.

Books by Nirvana

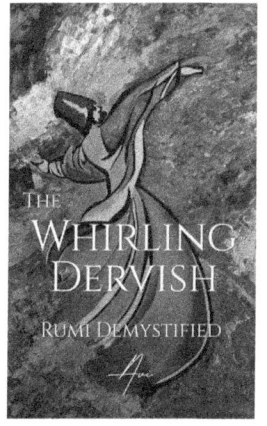

ISBN: 978-1962685009

ISBN: 979-8852311207

ISBN: 979-8392250196

ISBN: 979-8374196740

ISBN: 978-0578637068

ISBN: 978-1962685023

ISBN: 978-1962685047

ISBN: 978-1962685061

www.ingramcontent.com/pod-product-compliance
Lightning Source LLC
Chambersburg PA
CBHW031954080426
42735CB00007B/385